AF334173

GAME DAY
MICHIGAN FOOTBALL

GAME DAY
MICHIGAN FOOTBALL

*The Greatest Games, Players, Coaches and Teams
in the Glorious Tradition of Wolverine Football*

TRIUMPH BOOKS

CHICAGO

CONTENTS

FOREWORD BY BO SCHEMBECHLER   vii

INTRODUCTION   xi

TRADITIONS AND PAGEANTRY   1

THE GREATEST PLAYERS   21

THE GREAT COACHES   61

WOLVERINE SUPERLATIVES   73

THE RIVALRIES   103

TALKIN' MICHIGAN FOOTBALL   127

FACTS AND FIGURES   141

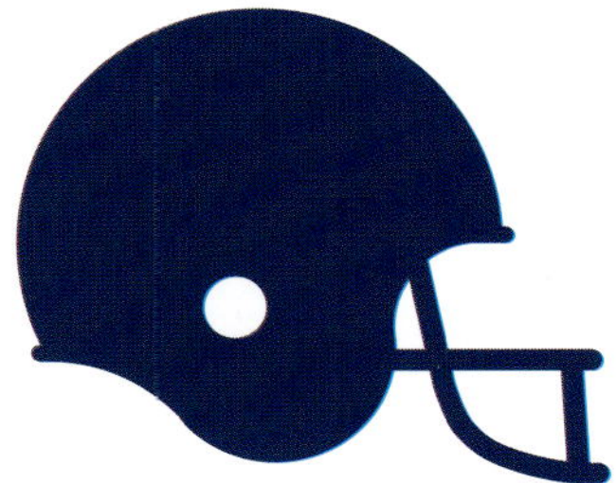

Foreword

In times of change, those brave enough to stay the course will be victors in the end.

There's no question that college football today is played on a landscape of radical change. Some is good. But some, I believe, undermines the very essence of what the game is all about.

All around the country, the word tradition is thrown around like a pocketful of dirty pennies.

That's a shame! *Tradition* is a precious word. It belongs only to the strongest who conduct themselves with honesty, integrity, and commitment to withstand every test of time.

That's Michigan football!

The legendary Fritz Crisler summed it up best more than 60 years ago: "Tradition is something you can't bottle. You can't buy it at the corner store. But it is there to sustain you when you need it most.

"I've called upon it time and time again. And so have countless other Michigan athletes and coaches. There is nothing like it. I hope it never dies."

That was true before Fritz Crisler got to Michigan. It was true all the time he was here. And it's just as true today as the day he said it.

There are excellent football programs in every part of our country. Most conduct themselves honorably and contribute to the overall tradition of real college football.

But how can anyone come close to the tradition in Ann Arbor, where games have been played since 1879?

More victories than any school anywhere in the country; around 111,000 fans for each game at the Big House; the most distinct helmet in the country; the greatest fight song in the history of college sports; with Ohio State, the most celebrated rivalry in all of sports; New Year's Day bowl games; Big Ten championships; the tunnel; the Little Brown Jug; the marching band; the tailgate parties.

And always remember: the University of Michigan is one of the most academically acclaimed state institutions in the nation and sits on one of the most colorful campus settings anywhere.

The history is alive and endless. But the essence of tradition transcends victories, statistics, events, and all the other celebrated features that comprise college football.

The essence of tradition lies in the hearts of the people who protect and perpetuate the storied history that was handed down to them; the storied history they carefully pass down to generations yet to come; the storied history you'll read about in the pages of this fascinating new book.

—Bo Schembechler

Introduction

In its 127 years of intercollegiate competition, the University of Michigan has won more football games (849) than any other program in Division I-A. No other program has won more conference titles than Michigan's 42 in the Big Ten, and Michigan's 11 national titles tie the school for fourth all-time. The Wolverines have appeared in bowl games for the last 31 years in a row.

When it comes to college football, nobody's done it better or for longer than the University of Michigan has. From Fielding Yost's point-a-minute teams to Bennie Oosterbaan and the 1948 champs, to Bo Schembechler's storied run as coach of the Wolverines, to the Heisman campaigns of Tom Harmon, Desmond Howard and Charles Woodson, to the 1997 National Championship, the Michigan program is more than an important part of college football history. It *is* college football history.

On the pages that follow, we present a snapshot of the traditions, the memories, the indelible images that make up the tapestry of Michigan football. So, as the storied fight song puts it so eloquently, "Hail! To the victors valiant."

TRADITIONS AND PAGEANTRY

It's logical that over 127 years of competition, some treasured and unique traditions would arise at Michigan. And they have — from the famed winged helmet, to the sprawling stadium known around the world as the Big House, to the best-known and most beloved fight song in college athletics.

Taken collectively, these are more than traditions. They're the very fabric of a university, the pride of a worldwide community of those who bleed maize and blue.

The winning tradition, rivalries and championships are not the only things that make University of Michigan football distinct. It's also the look, the sounds and the atmosphere that set the Wolverines apart from their college football peers.

The Colors

The school's official colors, Maize and Blue, have been around longer than the football program. A committee of students in the literary department selected the colors in 1867. The colors worn by Michigan's athletic teams were unofficially selected as deep blue and bright yellow by the Athletic Association in the early 1900s. The uniforms have undergone changes over the years, but the football team began wearing blue jerseys in 1927 and added white 'away' jerseys in 1949. Player names were added to the jerseys beginning in 1980.

The Helmet

Legendary coach Fritz Crisler was responsible for the most recognizable helmet in college football. When Crisler took over as head coach in 1938, he replaced the team's then-black helmets with the winged design featuring the school's Maize and Blue colors. Crisler added the winged design "to dress it up a little," he claimed. But the new look was not just for styling. Crisler felt it would aid his quarterbacks in finding receivers down the field. It had an immediate effect, as the Wolverines doubled their passing yards and sliced their interceptions nearly in half the first year they wore the redesigned helmets.

Wolverines

How Michigan acquired the nickname "Wolverines" is shrouded in mystery. As far as anyone knows, the ferocious carnivore is not indigenous to the state, but Michiganders have carried the moniker at least since the border dispute with Ohio known as the "Toledo War" in 1803. Researchers have speculated that its origin dates back to the days of the fur trade, when Sault Ste. Marie served as a hub for wolverine pelts in the 1700s. In 1927, a pair of wolverines named Bennie and Biff were paraded around Michigan Stadium in cages on game days. But their nasty dispositions led to their retirement after just one season.

The Band

The biggest unit representing the school at football games is not the team but the band. The University of Michigan Marching Band typically consists of 225 people and has been part of the school's tradition longer than the team. It was originally formed in 1844 and began performing at football games in 1899. They were nicknamed "The Transcontinental Band" after performing at Yankee Stadium and the Rose Bowl during the 1950 season.

The marching band was also the first from the collegiate ranks to perform at the Super Bowl, in 1973.

It was the Michigan Band that originated the "Script Ohio," which it introduced to the world on Oct. 15, 1932 in Columbus, Ohio, to honor its Ohio State hosts that day. The inaugural Sudler Trophy, awarded annually to the nation's top college marching band, was bestowed upon the Michigan Marching Band in 1983.

—— The Victors ——

Naturally, a Michigan victory was the inspiration for its unforgettable fight song. Louis Elbel attended Michigan's 12–11 conference championship victory over Chicago in 1898 and left Chicago's Marshall Field feeling the school needed a proper victory song. The Michigan Band played "Hot Time in the Old Town," and Elbel, a U-M music student, felt it didn't measure up to the moment. The melody for "The Victors" popped into his head as he walked home that day. He composed the song on the piano the following evening and changed the song into a march while taking a train to Ann Arbor. At the urging of his brother, Elbel had band arranger E.R. Schremser prepare song sheets for 23 instruments. John Philip Sousa and his band were the first to play the song, and the marching band adopted the song to celebrate athletic victories in May 1899.

"The Victors"

Hail! To the victors valiant

Hail! To the conqu'ring heroes

Hail! Hail! To Michigan

The leaders and the best

Hail! To the victors valiant

Hail! To the conqu'ring heroes

Hail! Hail! To Michigan

The champions of the West!

Michigan Stadium

The "Big House" has been the home of Michigan football since 1927. Originally seating 72,000 spectators, the stadium was built with 440 tons of reinforcing steel and 31,000 square feet of wire mesh on land that had once been home to a barn, a strawberry patch and an underground spring. Coach Fielding Yost had the foresight during the planning stages to allow for expansion.

Michigan defeated Ohio Wesleyan 33–0 in the first game at Michigan Stadium on Oct. 1, 1927, but the stadium was actually dedicated on Oct. 22, 1927, with a 21–0 victory over Ohio State. The facility was filled to capacity with 84,401 in attendance for the event.

Over the years, the seating capacity grew to its current 107,501. Michigan set an NCAA single-game attendance record in 2003 when 112,118 fans jammed the stadium to watch the Wolverines defeat Ohio State 35–21.

STADIUM
BLUE

MICHIGAN

—— Game Day ——

The Michigan Marching Band leads the way from campus to the stadium entrance before each home game, with a thousand or more fans in its wake. The golf course across from the stadium is premium tailgating real estate. Fans climb up over a hundred rows of seats in Michigan Stadium, the nation's largest football stadium, to take their places and await the arrival of their team. As game time approaches, the players burst from the tunnel and run onto the field under the Michigan Football banner. Players and cheerleaders alike jump up to touch it as they stream underneath.

Bob Ufer

As much as Fielding Yost, as much as Bo Schembechler, as much as Bennie Friedman or Tom Harmon or Desmond Howard — Bob Ufer is a revered Michigan icon. The voice of Michigan Football from 1945 through 1981, Ufer was the most blatant "homer" in broadcasting annals, and he made no apologies for it. For televised Michigan games, fans across the state would mute their TVs and listen to Ufer's call. After every Michigan score he sounded a horn that came from General George Patton's jeep. His impassioned, emotional calls excited fans like no one else could.

Among many colorful "Uferisms" are his description of a back "running like a penguin with a hot herring in his cummerbun." He referred to Woody Hayes and Ohio State as "Doctor StrangeHayes and his Scarlet and

Gray Legions." It was Ufer who coined the term "Mee-chigan." Not to mention "God bless your cotton-pickin' Maize and Blue hearts."

Ufer, a world-class middle distance runner as a Michigan student in the early 1940s, broadcast 362 games from 1945 until he died of cancer in 1981.

"Prejudiced? Partial?" Ufer would often say. "You better believe it. Michigan football is a religion and Saturday's the holy day of obligation."

Here's a sample of memorable Uferisms:

"That whirling dervish, Gordie Bell, who could run 15 minutes in a phone booth... and he wouldn't even touch the sides." (1975)

"Running through that Buckeye line like a bull with a bee in his ear."

—Describing Russell Davis in 1976

"General Bo's gonna stay on the ground now. There's no Luftwaffe; he's got the tanks in." —Describing a Bo Schembechler team with a late lead

"Michigan can't lose. They can only beat themselves."

"The hole that Yost dug, Canham carpeted, and Schembechler filled."

—On Michigan Stadium

Jim Harbaugh

"Old 98" Tom Harmon

THE GREATEST PLAYERS

Michigan's roster of greats reads like a who's who of college football legends. The names are familiar to fans of college football, and for the fans of Michigan's rivals, they still bring a shiver of dread. Here are some of the stars who have shone brightest during their tenures in Ann Arbor.

Michigan has had so many national award winners, so many great players, that they can't all be included here, which is why the following list should be considered representative, not definitive.

NEIL SNOW
(End–Fullback, 1898–1901)

Neil Snow played both fullback and end at Michigan. He was an All-American and captain of Fielding H. Yost's 1901 team as a senior. He capped off his playing career by scoring five touchdowns in the Wolverines' 49–0 rout of Stanford in the inaugural Tournament of Roses game, known today as the Rose Bowl.

WILLIE HESTON
(Halfback, 1901–1904)

Willie Heston was the spearhead of Yost's point-a-minute juggernauts. During Heston's playing career, the Wolverines won four national titles. In his time, no other ball-carrier could rival him. All four members on what Yost referred to as his "Heston Backfield" were explosive open-field runners, but Heston was unstoppable. The left halfback played for Michigan teams that scored 2,326 points to their opponents' 40 and never lost a game over four years. Heston scored 93 touchdowns in his brilliant career.

"There have been great centers through every year of American football, but the greatest center I ever saw was Germany Schulz ... one of the fastest big men on any field." **—GRANTLAND RICE**

ADOLPH "GERMANY" SCHULZ
(Center, 1904–1908)

Germany Schulz was the center on Grantland Rice's all-time team. Schulz dominated games on both sides on the line of scrimmage, backing up the line on defense. He was a 1907 All-American and a member of the AP All-Time team picked in 1951.

ALBERT BENBROOK
(Guard, 1908–1910)

Albert Benbrook was the first of the great pulling guards. At 240 pounds—a giant for his day—Benbrook could outrun most backs. He was a two-time All-American of whom Walter Camp remarked, "He leads his mates across the line with his quick, ripping charge that simply smothers the opposition."

HARRY KIPKE
(Halfback, 1921–1923)

Harry Kipke earned three letters at Michigan in football, basketball and baseball. On the gridiron he was an All-America halfback in 1922. Kipke excelled as a ball carrier, passer, blocker and kicker, and he was a terrific defensive player. He was also the best punter in the nation during the early 1920s. He was captain of the 8–0 national champion Wolverines as a senior in 1923, and he later returned to Ann Arbor as head coach of his alma mater from 1929 to 1937.

"In Benny Friedman, I have one of the greatest passers and smartest quarterbacks in history. He never makes a mistake." —FIELDING YOST

BENNY FRIEDMAN
(Quarterback, 1923–1926)

Friedman, a charter member of the College Football Hall of Fame, was the greatest passer of his day. George Little, a Fielding Yost assistant, left to become head coach at Wisconsin before Friedman's senior year. "I should have waited until Benny graduated," Little said. "In my first year as head coach at Madison, we lost only one game—to Michigan, 21–0. And Benny figured in all of the touchdowns. He was unstoppable." Friedman was a two-year All-American, in 1925 and '26.

BENNIE OOSTERBAAN
(End, 1924–1927)

The most interesting fact about Oosterbaan is that in 1948 he became the only man to win a national championship in his first year as a head coach, and he held that distinction for 53 years, until 2001. As a player, Oosterbaan was the finest pass receiver of his time. He was a three-time All-American, in 1925, '26, and '27, and was chosen on the All-Time All-America team in 1951. The Friedman-to-Oosterbaan connection was one of the most feared passing combos in history, and on defense, Oosterbaan consistently frustrated opposing ball carriers trying his end, including Red Grange.

THE WISTERTS

Francis, Albert and Alvin Wistert are the only threesome of brothers to all be named first-team All-America. All three were tackles, and all three wore the No. 11 jersey, which has since been retired in their honor. Francis "Whitey" Wistert was an All-American as a senior in 1933, when coach Harry Kipke's Wolverines won the national championship. In Francis' four years, Michigan posted a record of 31–1–3. Albert, also known as the "Ox," was an All-American and team MVP in 1942, then went on to an all-pro career with the Philadelphia Eagles. Alvin "Moose" Wistert was the oldest Michigan football player ever, thanks in large part to a four-year stint in the Marines during World War II before enrolling in 1946. Alvin was a two-time All-American, in 1948 and '49.

TOM HARMON
(Halfback, 1938–1940)

Tom Harmon teamed with quarterback Forest Evashevski to lift the Wolverines out of the football doldrums in the years immediately preceding World War II. Harmon led the nation in scoring in 1939 and 1940, finished second in Heisman balloting in 1939 and won the Heisman Trophy in 1940. Over his three seasons in Ann Arbor, Harmon ran for 2,134 yards, scored 33 touchdowns and threw 16 touchdown passes. In his last game for the Maize and Blue—the 1940 Ohio State showdown—"Old 98" rushed for 139 yards and two touchdowns, completed 11 of 12 passes for 151 yards and two more touchdowns, intercepted three passes, running one back for a score, and averaged 50 yards per punt, in a 40–0 Wolverine win. After a thrilling career as a pilot in World War II, Harmon married film star Elyse Knox and became one of the nation's top sports broadcasters and directors.

"He was better than Red Grange,

the 'Galloping Ghost.' Tom could do more things. He ran, passed, punted, blocked, kicked off and kicked extra points and field goals. He was a superb defensive player." —**MICHIGAN COACH FRITZ CRISLER ON HARMON**

"You have to smell where to go on pass defense— and my sniffer's not too good."

—CHAPPUIS ON HIS ONLY WEAKNESS, PASS DEFENSE

BOB CHAPPUIS
(Halfback, 1942, 1946–1947)

Bob Chappuis had his football career interrupted by World War II—an aerial gunner, he was shot down on a mission over Italy and later escaped captivity—and picked up right where he left off in 1946. A true triple-threat halfback, Chappuis was an All-American and Heisman Trophy runner-up in 1947 for coach Fritz Crisler's national champs. On New Year's Day 1948, Chappuis set two Rose Bowl records, for total offense and pass completions.

CHALMERS "BUMP" ELLIOTT
(Halfback, 1946–1947)

Chappuis wasn't the only All-America halfback for the 1947 Wolverines; Bump Elliott joined him in the honor. Crisler called Elliott the greatest right halfback he ever saw. He led the Big Nine in scoring as a senior with 54 points and was named the conference's MVP. He later returned to Michigan as head coach and led the Maize and Blue to the Big Ten and Rose Bowl titles in 1964.

***"To top off his marvelous physical gifts of size and speed and strength,** plus an uncanny coordination, Kramer was one of the fiercest competitors I've ever seen. Nothing was impossible for him—the impossible was only a challenge."* —KRAMER'S COACH, BENNIE OOSTERBAAN

RON KRAMER
(End, 1954–1956)

Ron Kramer earned nine letters at Michigan— three each in football, basketball and track. He led both the football team and the basketball team in scoring for two seasons. He was a standout on both sides of the ball, and he was particularly dangerous as a receiver. A 230-pound high-jumper in track, Kramer was a consensus All-America end for two years (1955 and '56). His football jersey No. 87 was retired following his senior year, and he went on to an all-pro career with Vince Lombardi's Green Bay Packers in the early 1960s.

BOB TIMBERLAKE
(Quarterback, 1962–1964)

Tall, talented Bob Timberlake quarterbacked Michigan to the Big Ten and Rose Bowl titles in 1964. He was MVP of the Big Ten, consensus All-America and finished fourth in that year's Heisman voting.

BILL YEARBY
(Tackle, 1963–1965)

Bill Yearby was one of the best defensive tackles in the nation in the mid-1960s. He was blessed with both strength and great speed, and he was best known for his prowess in pursuit. Yearby was named an All-American in 1964 and '65.

RON JOHNSON
(Halfback, 1966–1968)

During his three-year college career, Ron Johnson virtually rewrote the Michigan rushing record book. Among the school standards he set were those for single-season and career rushing yardage. He also left Ann Arbor with eight new Big Ten marks. Johnson was two-time team MVP and was an All-American and Big Ten MVP in 1968. The 347 yards he gained against Wisconsin in 1968 set an NCAA record at the time.

THOMAS CURTIS
(Defensive Back, 1967–1969)

In the late 1960s, a dangerous pass by a Michigan opponent could be defined as any aerial thrown in the direction of Thomas Curtis. During his three-year career with the Wolverines, Curtis intercepted 25 passes. He started off quickly in his career, tying a then–Big Ten record with seven interceptions. He broke that record the following season with 10 takeaways and had eight more as a senior during Bo Schembechler's first season as head coach in 1969. Curtis also made 45 unassisted tackles and was named an All-American as a senior. The 6'1" Curtis was a two-time Big Ten first team selection and set a then-NCAA record with 431 return yards on his interceptions.

DAN DIERDORF
(Offensive Tackle, 1968–1970)

Dan Dierdorf was a two-time All–Big Ten and 1970 All-America offensive tackle. After his college career, Dierdorf went on to an all-pro career with the St. Louis Cardinals and was twice named the NFL's top offensive lineman.

REGGIE McKENZIE
(Offensive Guard, 1969–1971)

A consensus All-American as a senior in 1971, Reggie McKenzie is recognized as one of the game's greatest pulling guards. McKenzie helped clear the way for the Wolverines to two Big Ten titles and Rose Bowl appearances.

BILLY TAYLOR
(Halfback, 1969–1971)

Billy Taylor was MVP of the 1971 Big Ten champion Wolverine team that finished with a perfect 11–0 regular season before dropping the Rose Bowl by one point. He exited Michigan after his senior year with the school's career rushing record of 3,072 yards, and second only to Tom Harmon with 32 touchdowns. Taylor was a three-time All–Big Ten selection and a 1971 All-American.

THOM DARDEN
(Defensive Back, 1969–1971)

One of the best punt returners in Michigan history, Darden was a three-year regular in the defensive backfield, starting and excelling at all four positions. Of his 11 career interceptions, Darden notched touchdown returns of 92 and 60 yards.

DAVE BROWN
(Defensive Halfback, 1972–1974)

Brown intercepted nine passes in his college career and also has an 88-yard punt return to his credit. He was co-captain of Bo Schembechler's 1974 Big Ten champs, was a three-time all-conference pick and a two-year All-American, in 1973 and '74.

ROB LYTLE
(Running Back, 1974–1976)

A consensus All-American, the Big Ten's MVP and third-highest Heisman vote-getter in 1976, Rob Lytle left Michigan after his senior year in possession of the school records for rushing in a single season and career. In the 1976 Michigan State game, Lytle averaged 18 yards on 10 carries.

MARK DONAHUE
(Offensive Guard, 1975–1977)

Donahue was a two-time consensus All-American—the 13th Michigan player to be so honored twice—and was one of the greatest pulling guards in school history.

Three Michigan greats in peak form: Mark Donahue (60) opens a gaping hole for running back Rob Lytle after a handoff from Rick Leach (7).

RICK LEACH
(Quarterback, 1975–1978)

Rick Leach, a gunslinging southpaw who played in the mid- to late-1970s, broke all of Michigan's career passing, total offense and touchdown records that had stood before him.

He was All–Big Ten for three years, and in his senior year—1978—he was an All-American, finished third in the Heisman voting and was named the Big Ten's MVP.

ANTHONY CARTER
(Wide Receiver, 1979–1982)

The Big Ten hadn't had a three-time All-American in 36 years, until Michigan wide receiver Anthony Carter pulled it off in 1980, '81 and '82. He was the first 3,000-yard pass receiver in conference history. During his time in Ann Arbor, Carter caught 161 passes for 3,076 yards and 37 touchdowns and scored 40 touchdowns in all. He set an NCAA all-purpose running mark with a 17.4-yard average. His senior year, he finished fourth in the Heisman Trophy balloting.

"The best player I ever coached." —BO SCHEMBECHLER

Anthony Carter caught 37 touchdown passes in his brilliant Michigan career.

JOHN ELLIOTT
(Offensive Tackle, 1984–1987)

John "Jumbo" Elliott was a four-year starting offensive tackle and a two-year consensus All-American. He was a first-round pick in the 1988 NFL Draft and enjoyed a 14-year pro career with the New York Giants and Jets.

Jumbo Elliott was a rugged two-time All-American at tackle.

Jim Harbaugh
(Quarterback, 1983–1986)

Quarterback Jim Harbaugh completely rewrote Michigan's passing record book. He led the nation in pass efficiency in 1985, and his 2,729 passing yards in 1986 was a school record that stood until 2002. He quarterbacked the Wolverines to a Fiesta Bowl victory following the 1985 season and the Big Ten title in 1986. As a senior in '86, Harbaugh was chosen Big Ten Player of the Year and finished third in the Heisman voting.

MARK MESSNER
(Defensive Tackle, 1985–1988)

Messner was a two-year All-America defensive tackle who graduated from Michigan with more tackles for loss (70) for more lost yardage (376) than anyone who had gone before him. Messner started all 49 games of his college career and led the Wolverines in sacks three straight years.

Mark Messner harassed opposing quarterbacks for four years, posting 36 sacks for 273 yards in losses.

TRIPP WELBORNE
(Safety, 1987–1990)

After converting from wide receiver to defensive back following his freshman year, Sullivan A. "Tripp" Welborne notched nine career interceptions and 238 tackles. He was a record-breaking punt returner and a two-year All-American, in 1989 and 1990.

"Hello, Heisman!" — ABC's KEITH JACKSON, UPON WATCHING HOWARD'S 93-YARD PUNT RETURN VS. OHIO STATE AND FAMOUS HEISMAN POSE IN THE END ZONE

DESMOND HOWARD
(Wide Receiver, 1989–1991)

In 1991, Desmond Howard became Michigan's second Heisman Trophy winner, joining Tom Harmon on the list. Howard was the most electrifying player in college football in his day. He was the first receiver ever to lead the Big Ten in scoring, and he set a handful of NCAA records in the process. He received more first-place Heisman votes than anyone else before him and also captured the Walter Camp and Maxwell Awards as a junior.

GREG SKREPENAK
(Offensive Tackle, 1988–1991)

Greg Skrepenak was a four-year starting offensive tackle for the Wolverines, and his 48 consecutive starts were at the time a school record. He was a two-year All-American and a finalist for both the Outland Trophy and Lombardi Award.

USC
SKREPENAK
75

"You know what feeling you get when you win. You know what feeling you get when you lose. You learn that early on. You either get used to the feeling of losing, or you do something to win." —CHARLES WOODSON

CHARLES WOODSON
(Cornerback, Receiver, 1995–1997)

In 1997, Michigan's Charles Woodson became the first primarily defensive player ever to win the Heisman Trophy. He took over as a starter in the second game of his freshman year and never relinquished the job. He was named Big Ten Player of the Year twice. As a junior in 1997, Woodson picked off eight enemy aerials and was voted MVP of Michigan's national champions. He cemented his legend against Ohio State—he was on the field for a staggering 83 plays in the 20–14 win over the No. 4 Buckeyes, and he clinched his Heisman Trophy with a 78-yard punt return for a score and an interception in the end zone that ended a late Buckeye drive.

STEVE HUTCHINSON
(Guard, 1997–2000)

Steve Hutchinson was a four-year starter at guard and a two-time team captain. He was first-team All–Big Ten four straight years, did not allow a sack in either of his final two seasons and was a two-year All-American.

BRAYLON EDWARDS
(Wide Receiver, 2001–04)

Braylon Edwards believed it was his destiny to wear the prestigious No. 1 uniform. Son of former Michigan running back Stanley Edwards, Braylon Edwards finally convinced coach Lloyd Carr to give him that number after his sophomore season. Edwards traded in his No. 80 uniform and proved his worthiness of wearing No. 1, setting school records for career receptions (252), receiving yards (3,542), receiving touchdowns (39) and consecutive games with a reception (38). He won the Biletnikoff Award as the nation's outstanding wide receiver as a senior, catching 97 passes for 1,330 yards and 15 touchdowns.

"I almost cried. It was magnificent. I love my teammates to death and they never quit. They stood strong in the fourth quarter. We imposed our will on Michigan State in the second half. We had a never-say-die attitude and we refused to lose this game." —EDWARDS, AFTER SCORING THE GAME-WINNING TD IN MICHIGAN'S STUNNING 45–37 THREE-OVERTIME WIN OVER MICHIGAN STATE

——— UM's Position Tradition ———

With a legacy of greatness at every position, Michigan can point with special pride to the recent impact that Wolverines have had at three important positions.

Quarterbacks

The pressure on a Michigan quarterback is enormous. In a program where losing isn't tolerated, the starting quarterback must handle harsh scrutiny and tough critics as well as onrushing linemen.

It takes a special player to grasp that responsibility. No wonder so many Wolverine signal-callers have made a seamless transition to the National Football League.

Every starting Michigan quarterback since 1990 has graduated to the next level. New England's Tom Brady, a sixth-round draft pick who completed his Michigan career in 1999, stands above that group. He has led the Patriots to three Super Bowl championships and is considered one of the game's elite players.

Elvis Grbac, Todd Collins, Brian Griese, Scott Dreisbach, Drew Henson and John Navarre also carried their skills to the highest level of football. Navarre, a three-year starter from 2001 to 2003, holds most of the school's career passing records, including passing yards (9,254), completions (765) and attempts (1,366).

Jim Harbaugh (1983–86) was the Chicago Bears' No. 1 draft choice in 1987 and had a distinguished pro career with the Bears, Indianapolis Colts, Baltimore Ravens, San Diego Chargers and Carolina Panthers until his retirement in 2001.

In the 1970s, Rick Leach broke Big Ten records for total offense and touchdown passes and was named the All–Big Ten quarterback three times.

Elvis Grbac was one of a long line of brilliant Wolverine signal-callers.

Offensive Linemen

Though most football fans now know him as a broadcaster, Dan Dierdorf was one of the greatest players to wear a Michigan uniform. He was a consensus All-American in 1970 and became one of the NFL's premier offensive tackles with the St. Louis Cardinals. He was twice named the league's best offensive lineman, was elected to six Pro Bowls and was inducted into the Pro Football Hall of Fame in 1996.

Dierdorf is just one of many dominant offensive linemen to come through the program. Reggie McKenzie, a consensus All-American in 1971, played 11 seasons in the NFL. Tackles Paul Seymour, Mike Kenn and Jon Giesler were first-round NFL draft picks during the 1970s.

Bubba Paris won Super Bowl championships during the following decade while blocking for Joe Montana and the San Francisco 49ers. John "Jumbo" Elliott won a Super Bowl ring as a member of the New York Giants in 1991.

Steve Everitt was the 14th overall player selected in the 1993 draft by the Cleveland Browns, the first Wolverines center ever chosen that high. Tackles Jon Runyan (1993–95) and Jon Jansen (1995–98) have excelled in the pros after earning All-America accolades at Michigan.

In 2001, four-year starters Steve Hutchinson and Jeff Backus were chosen back-to-back in the first round by the Seattle Seahawks and Detroit Lions, respectively. Hutchinson, a two-time All-American, has blossomed into a Pro Bowl guard with the Seahawks.

The most memorable Michigan lineman never played in the NFL. Former president Gerald Ford was the team's MVP in 1934.

Gerald Ford

Desmond Howard

Wide Receivers

There's no need to give their full names. Just throw out the initials A.C. and the first names Desmond and Braylon and every Michigan fan knows who you're talking about.

Anthony Carter, Desmond Howard and Braylon Edwards provided enough thrills and spectacular plays during their Wolverine careers to fill up a highlight reel by themselves. Carter became the first Big Ten player in 36 years to earn All-American honors three consecutive seasons from 1980 to 1982. Carter broke every Michigan receiving, kick returning and scoring record during his career. A Heisman finalist in 1982, Carter played 14 professional seasons and was voted to the Pro Bowl in 1987 and 1988. His finest moment as a pro came during the 1987 postseason, when he caught 10 passes for 227 yards against the heavily favored Niners in Minnesota's playoff upset of San Francisco.

Howard, just 5'9" tall, became the first receiver to lead the conference in scoring in 1991. He won the Heisman Trophy in a landslide, collecting the most first-place votes ever, after setting 12 single-season school records. Howard was a first-round draft pick by the

Washington Redskins and went on to become the MVP of Super Bowl XXXI while playing for the Green Bay Packers.

Edwards (2001–04) used his length (6'3") and strength to set the school's career records for receptions, receiving yards and receiving touchdowns. In his senior season, Edwards won the Biletnikoff Award as the nation's top wide receiver. Edwards was selected by the Cleveland Browns in the first round of the 2005 draft.

Derrick Alexander (1989–93), who ranks in the top 10 in several Michigan receiving categories, had a successful pro career with four NFL teams. Amani Toomer (1992–95) has played for the New York Giants since 1996.

THE GREAT COACHES

Michigan has been blessed with some of the game's greatest tacticians, motivators and leaders. These names rise to the top of the list.

Fielding H. Yost
1901-1926

Fielding H. "Hurry Up" Yost came to Michigan from Stanford in 1901 as a result of the Pacific Coast Conference's adoption of a rule forbidding its schools to employ non-alumni as coaches. Yost took his first Michigan team out to California to play Stanford in the first-ever Rose Bowl game, on Jan 1, 1902, and whipped his old employer 49–0. Yost coached 25 seasons at Michigan, 1901-1926 with a one-year hiatus in 1924, and compiled a record of 165–29–10. He earned his nickname from his constant exhortations to his players in practice to "Hurry up! Hurry up!" He won his reputation as a legend by coaching his immortal point-a-minute teams of 1901-1905 to four national championships in five years. Eight of his Michigan teams finished unbeaten. Yost also served as Michigan's Director of Athletics from 1921 to 1941.

YOST AT MICHIGAN

YEAR	OVERALL	BIG TEN/PLACE	BOWL
1901	11–0*	4–0/1st	Rose
1902	11–0*	5–0/1st	
1903	11–0–1*	3–0–1/1st	
1904	10–0*	2–0/1st	
1905	12–1	2–1/2nd	
1906	4–1	1–0/1st	
1907	5–1	N/A	
1908	5–2–1	N/A	
1909	6–1	N/A	
1910	3–0–3	N/A	
1911	5–1–2	N/A	
1912	5–2	N/A	
1913	6–1	N/A	
1914	6–3	N/A	
1915	4–3–1	N/A	
1916	7–2	N/A	
1917	8–2	0–1/8th	
1918	5–0*	2–0/1st	
1919	3–4	1–4/7th	
1920	5–2	2–2/6th	
1921	5–1–1	2–1–1/5th	
1922	6–0–1	4–0/1st	
1923	8–0*	4–0/1st	
1925	7–1	5–1/1st	
1926	7–1	5–0/1st	
Total	165–29–10 (.833)	42–10–2 (.778)	

*Claimed National Championship

*"**Tradition is something you can't bottle.***

You can't buy it at the corner store. But it is there to sustain

you when you need it most. I've called upon it time and time

again. And so have countless other Michigan athletes and

coaches. There is nothing like it. I hope it never dies."

—FRITZ CRISLER

Herbert O. "Fritz" Crisler
1938-1947

Fritz Crisler's winning percentage of .805 (71–16–3) over his 10 years from 1938-1947 ranks second in school history (minimum of 50 games coached) behind only Yost's .833. His 1947 team finished 10–0, won the national title and beat USC 49–0 in the Rose Bowl. Crisler played football at the University of Chicago under Amos Alonzo Stagg and stayed on at Chicago as a Stagg assistant for eight years. He held head coaching positions at Minnesota and Princeton before bringing his innovative approach—and the winged helmet—to Ann Arbor. At a time when most teams were switching to the T-formation, Crisler stuck faithfully to the single wing. His buck lateral and spinner-cycle offense, requiring flawless timing, ball-handling and execution, was a thrill to watch.

"On offense, it's poise, finesse, determination. On defense, it's fury, fight, utter abandon." **—CRISLER, ON HIS FOOTBALL PHILOSOPHY**

CRISLER AT MICHIGAN

YEAR	OVERALL	BIG TEN/PLACE	BOWL
1938	6–1–1	3–1–1/2nd	
1939	6–2	3–2/4th	
1940	7–1	3–1/2nd	
1941	6–1–1	3–1–1/2nd	
1942	7–3	3–2/3rd	
1943	8–1	6–0/1st	
1944	8–2	5–2/2nd	
1945	7–3	5–1/2nd	
1946	6–2–1	5–1–1/2nd	
1947	10–0*	6–0/1st	Rose
Total	71–16–3 (.805)	42–11–3 (.777)	

*Awarded AP national championship after bowl game

Glenn E. "Bo" Schembechler
1969-1989

Though he hasn't roamed the sidelines at Michigan Stadium since 1989, Glenn "Bo" Schembechler remains perhaps the most recognizable coach in the state. Tough, blunt, opinionated and wildly successful, Schembechler built a legacy that will never be forgotten.

During his 21 seasons as Michigan's head coach, Schembechler led the Wolverines to 13 Big Ten championships, 10 Rose Bowls and 194 wins. The victory total is unmatched by any other Michigan football coach.

Hard to believe, but there was actually a time when the name 'Schembechler' did not reverberate in the minds of the Michigan faithful. When Schembechler was named head coach prior to the 1969 season, no one knew what to expect from the former Woody Hayes assistant.

Schembechler had been plying his trade in relative anonymity as head coach at his alma mater, Miami of Ohio, for six seasons.

"There weren't many people out there who knew anything about Schembechler," he related to former player Jim Brandstatter in *Tales from Michigan Stadium.* "It certainly wasn't a household word!"

He became a household word for both Wolverines and Ohio State fans in his first year as head coach when Michigan stunned the No. 1 ranked Buckeyes 24–12. That victory earned him three Coach of the Year awards.

Schembechler's hard-driving style didn't suit every player, but that never bothered him.

He hung a sign in the Michigan locker room that read "Those who stay will be champions." And in most seasons, those encouraging words came to fruition.

During the 1970s, the Wolverines had a nation-best 96–10–3 mark. Michigan never had a losing record in the 1980s, either, before Schembechler retired for health reasons. He served as the school's Director of Athletics between 1988 and 1990 and the school's football offices are named after him. When he retired in 1989, Schembechler was the fifth-winningest coach in Division I-A history, with 234 career victories.

SCHEMBECHLER AT MICHIGAN

YEAR	OVERALL	BIG TEN/PLACE	BOWL
1938	6–1–1	3–1–1/2nd	
1969	8–3	6–1/1st*	Rose
1970	9–1	6–1/2nd	
1971	11–1	8–0/1st	Rose
1972	10–1	7–1/1st*	
1973	10–0–1	7–0–1/1st*	
1974	10–1	7–1/1st*	
1975	8–2–2	7–1/2nd	Orange
1976	10–2	7–1/1st*	Rose
1977	10–2	7–1/1st*	Rose
1978	10–2	7–1/1st*	Rose
1979	8–4	6–2/3rd	Gator
1980	10–2	8–0/1st	Rose
1981	9–3	6–3/3rd	Bluebonnet
1982	8–4	8–1/1st	Rose
1983	9–3	8–1/2nd	Sugar
1984	6–6	5–4/6th	Holiday
1985	10–1–1	6–1–1/2nd	Fiesta
1986	11–2	7–1/1st	Rose
1987	8–4	5–3/4th	Hall of Fame
1988	9–2–1	7–0–1/1st	Rose
1989	10–2	8–0/1st	Rose
Total	194–48–5 (.796)	143–24–3 (.850)	

*Shared Conference championship

The end of an era: Bo Schembechler prowls the sidelines one final time as his Wolverines lose a tense battle to USC 17–10 in his final game.

Lloyd Carr
1995-present

Lloyd Carr saw his first Michigan football game in 1969, when he was an assistant high school coach at Detroit Nativity. Little did Carr know that he'd eventually become the face of Michigan football for more than a decade. Carr gradually climbed through the coaching ranks and landed at Michigan in 1980, when Bo Schembechler hired him as a defensive backs coach. He was the school's defensive coordinator for eight years before he was

named head coach prior to the 1995 season. In his third season in 1997, Carr led the team to a 12–0 record and the Associated Press national championship, earning him six national Coach of the Year awards. In 11 seasons as head coach, Carr has compiled a 102–34 record and led the team to three Rose Bowls, five Big Ten titles and five 10-win seasons. From 1997 to 2000, the Wolverines won four consecutive bowl games. In 2003, Carr joined Fielding Yost, Bennie Oosterbaan and Schembechler as the only Michigan head coaches to coach more than 100 games. As a Schembechler disciple, Carr still holds the tenets of defense and a strong rushing attack to heart, but his teams typically rank near the top of the Big Ten in passing offense.

"I think every guy who has played at Michigan takes great pride in this." —LLOYD CARR, ON THE 1997 NATIONAL CHAMPIONSHIP

CARR AT MICHIGAN

YEAR	OVERALL	BIG TEN/PLACE	BOWL
1995	9–4	5–3/3rd	Alamo
1996	8–4	5–3/5th	Outback
1997	12–0**	8–0/1st	Rose
1998	10–3	7–1/1st*	Citrus
1999	10–2	6–2/2nd	Orange
2000	9–3	6–2/1st*	Citrus
2001	8–4	6–2/2nd	Citrus
2002	10–3	6–2/3rd	Outback
2003	10–3	7–1/1st	Rose
2004	9–3	7–1/1st*	Rose
2005	7–5	5–3/3rd	Alamo
Total	102–34 (.750)	68–20 (.773)	

*Shared Conference championship
**National Champions

Glenn Doughty and the 1970 Wolverines ushered in a new era of Michigan football dominance.

WOLVERINE SUPERLATIVES

Michigan football history is littered with moments of greatness — National Championships won, great games played, superior individual efforts, memorable upsets and more. Here is a small sample of that record of achievement.

The Great Teams

1901–1905 (55–1–1)

Fielding H. "Hurry Up" Yost coached Michigan through the first quarter of the 20th century. His first five teams—his immortal "Point-a-Minute" teams—scored 2,821 points to their opponents' 42. From 1901 through 1904, Michigan did not lose a game and won the national title all four years. Yost chose his 1902 "Heston Backfield" as the best of his coaching tenure. With Willie Heston at left half, joined by halfbacks Albert Herrnstein and Everett Sweeley, fullback Neil Snow and Harrison

Weeks at quarterback, the '02 Wolverines outscored their opponents 644–12 on the way to an 11–0 record. The previous year, Yost's first at the helm in Ann Arbor, Michigan finished 11–0 with a 550–0 total score. On New Year's Day, 1902, Yost took his team out to California to play in the inaugural Tournament of Roses Game (now called the Rose Bowl) and beat his old employer, Stanford, 49–0. The game was so one-sided that 14 years passed before there was another one; it was replaced in the meantime by events such as ostrich races.

1923 (8–0)

Michigan captured the sixth national title of the Yost era in 1923, posting a perfect 8–0 mark for the season. Halfback Harry Kipke and center Jack Blott were All-Americans. Both would go on to coach Michigan to championships in later years—Kipke as head coach, Blott as line coach. The 1923 Wolverines outscored the opposition 150–12 and pitched five shutouts.

1933 (7–0–1)

Coach Harry Kipke brought a national title to his alma mater in 1933 behind All-America linemen in center Charles Bernard, whom pro coaches called the greatest college player in the country that year, and tackle Frances "Whitey" Wistert. Quarterback Stanley Fay served as team captain. Only a tie with Minnesota, who would go on to win the national championship the next year, marred an otherwise perfect record. The 1933 Wolverine defense never allowed more than six points all year and held five of eight opponents scoreless.

1940 (7–1)

The 1940 Wolverines finished third in the national rankings, their only blemish being a 7–6 loss to Minnesota, who went on to win the national championship that year. This was the squad that produced the first of Michigan's Heisman Trophy winners—halfback Tom Harmon. Fullback Bob Westfall and end Edward Frutig joined Harmon on that year's All-America selections. Only three opponents managed to score at all on that 1940 Michigan team, captained by quarterback Forest Evashevski.

1947 (10–0)

Few if any teams ever played offense with the precision and verve of Fritz Crisler's "Mad Magicians" of 1947. Their execution of the buck-lateral and spinner cycle out of the single-wing formation left opponents embarrassed and frustrated, often tackling two or three Michigan backs, none of whom had the ball. Having two All-America halfbacks—Bob Chappuis, the Heisman Trophy runner-up, and Chalmers "Bump" Elliott—didn't hurt. Led by tackle Alvin Wistert, end Len Ford and linebackers Dan Dworsky and Rick Kempthorn, the '47 Michigan defense pitched five shutouts and gave up a total of 53 points all year. Gene Derricotte was the nation's premier punt returner. The AP held a special post-bowl poll—a first—after Michigan's 49–0 throttling of USC in the Rose Bowl to replace Notre Dame with Michigan at the top spot.

1948 (9–0)

Crisler retired from coaching and left the team to Bennie Oosterbaan in 1948. With All-Americans in quarterback Pete Elliott, end Dick Rifenburg and tackle Alvin Wistert, the Wolverines extended their winning streak to 23 games, dating back to the middle of the 1946 season. Defensively there were five more shutouts and 44 total points surrendered. The Big Nine's no-repeat rule precluded a postseason trip, but Michigan repeated as national champion. Oosterbaan's national title in 1948 was the last by a first-year major-college head coach for 53 years.

1964 (9–1)

Bump Elliott, one of the famous Mad Magicians of 1947, was now head coach at his alma mater. Tall, talented Bob Timberlake was an All-America quarterback. On Oct. 17 against Purdue, Timberlake flew through the Boilermaker defense for a 54-yard touchdown run, cutting a 21–14 deficit to 21–20 with less than five minutes remaining. But Timberlake, the Big Ten's MVP that season, was stopped one foot short on the two-point try, leading to the only setback in an otherwise perfect season. With a 34–7 rout of Oregon State in the Rose Bowl, the 1964 Wolverines finished 9–1 and ranked No. 4 in both polls—one foot short of a national championship.

Bennie Oosterbaan's 1948 Wolverines, shown here against Illinois, were shut out of the Rose Bowl (thanks to the Big Nine's no-repeat rule) but not out of another national championship.

Their New Year's Day loss to USC notwithstanding, the 1976 Wolverines spent much of the season ranked No. 1 in the nation.

1970-1974 (50-4-1)

Bo Schembechler's Michigan teams of the early 1970s flirted with perfection, winning 50 of 55 games over five seasons. The star-studded units featured All-Americans in halfback Billy Taylor, offensive linemen Dan Dierdorf, Reggie McKenzie and Paul Seymour, defensive linemen David Gallagher and Henry Hill, linebackers Marty Huff and Mike Taylor, and defensive backs Thom Darden, Randy Logan and Dave Brown. The 1971 club took an 11–0 record to the Rose Bowl only to drop a one-point decision to Stanford.

1976 (10-2)

Michigan spent most of the 1976 season as the No. 1 team in the nation. The Wolverines were 8–0 on Nov. 6, when a 16–14 loss at Purdue dropped them from the top spot. Rob Lytle amassed 1,469 rushing yards at 6.65 yards per carry on his way to Big Ten MVP honors that fall. Rick Leach was in his sophomore year and etching his name in the school's quarterback lore. All-America linebacker Calvin O'Neal broke his own school record with 153 tackles after posting 151 the previous season. A 51–0 romp over Stanford in Game 2 and a 22–0 blanking of Ohio State punctuated the season, with the Wolverines finishing third in both polls.

Charles Woodson's scintillating Heisman season helped bring another national championship to Ann Arbor.

1997 (12–0)

The first national championship in half a century came Michigan's way in 1997. Cornerback Charles Woodson became the first primarily defensive player ever to win the Heisman Trophy. He intercepted eight passes for the Wolverines and also lent his electrifying skills to the offensive side of the ball and the punt return unit. Brian Griese piloted an offense that bristled with weapons such as running back Chris Howard and receiver Tai Streets. Tight end Jerame Tuman and defensive end Glen Steele were All-Americans. The Wolverines cemented their title with a 20–14 win over Ohio State to conclude the regular season and a 21–16 Rose Bowl triumph over Washington State.

The Bowls
Michigan's Greatest Bowl Game Perfomances

1902 ROSE BOWL
MICHIGAN 49, STANFORD 0

The Tournament of Roses had been celebrated on New Year's Day in Pasadena for more than a decade with a parade and various sporting events before a football game was added to the festivities in 1902. Michigan, "The Champion of the West," was invited to play Stanford, the Pacific champion, in that first Tournament of Roses football game. The crowd of 8,000 on hand at Tournament Park witnessed Michigan run for 527 yards to Stanford's 67 in the 49–0 rout. Halfback Willie Heston picked up 170 of Michigan's yards, with fullback Neil Snow scoring five touchdowns. The game was called with over eight minutes left to go as Stanford captain Ralph Fisher was delegated to concede the victory to the visitors. Michigan coach Fielding Yost had been let go as Stanford coach after the previous season because of a rule calling for Stanford grads exclusively to coach Stanford teams. The outcome was so lopsided that the Tournament of Roses committee replaced the football game with chariot races, ostrich races and polo for the next 14 years before football was resumed in 1916.

How dominant were Fritz Crisler's 1947 Wolverines in a 49–0 Rose Bowl shellacking of USC? After the game, the Associated Press took the unprecedented step of holding a post-bowl poll and awarding the national championship to Michigan.

1948 ROSE BOWL
MICHIGAN 49, SOUTHERN CALIFORNIA 0

Michigan's second bowl game, the 1948 Rose Bowl, ended like the first—in a 49–0 triumph. The victim this time was Southern California. Led by Heisman Trophy runner-up Bob Chappuis and Big Nine MVP Bump Elliott at the halfbacks, the Wolverines outgained the Trojans 491 yards to 133. Michigan scored in every quarter, took a 21–0 advantage into the locker room at halftime, and tacked on seven more points in the third period and 21 more in the fourth. Notre Dame was ranked No. 1 at the time and had beaten USC 38–7 to conclude the regular season, but the Associated Press held a special poll after the bowl games to oust Notre Dame from the top spot and replace the Irish with Michigan as 1947 National Champion.

1951 ROSE BOWL
MICHIGAN 14, CALIFORNIA 6

Michigan brought a 5–3–1 record to Pasadena to face fifth-ranked California in the 1951 Rose Bowl. Needless to say, the Golden Bears were favored to win. It was a tale of two halves. Cal outgained Michigan 192–65, racked up a 10–2 edge in first downs in the first half, and took a 6–0 lead by intermission. In the second half, coach Bennie Oosterbaan's Wolverines picked up 226 total yards and 15 first downs to 52 yards and 2 first downs for California. And in the most important stat, fullback Don Dufek ran for two Michigan touchdowns in the fourth quarter for the 14–6 win.

1965 ROSE BOWL
MICHIGAN 34, OREGON STATE 7

Michigan finished the 1964 regular season with an 8–1 record, the Big Ten title and a fourth-place national ranking. Oregon State came into Pasadena 8–2 and ranked eighth nationally. After a scoreless first period, the Beavers drew first blood early in the second on a five-yard TD pass from Paul Brothers to Doug McDougall. Later in the second quarter, Wolverine tailback Mel Anthony scored on an 84-yard run, opening the floodgates. A 43-yard touchdown gallop by Carl Ward put Michigan up 12–7 at the half. Game MVP Anthony scored twice more in the third quarter and quarterback Bob Timberlake tacked on a 24-yard touchdown run down the sideline in the fourth, and Michigan found itself 34–7 victors and 4–0 all-time in the postseason.

1981 ROSE BOWL
MICHIGAN 23, WASHINGTON 6

Michigan lost Games 2 and 3 of 1980 by a combined total of five points, then rattled off eight straight wins, including three consecutive shutouts, and traveled to Pasadena on New Year's Day having not surrendered a touchdown over the last 18 quarters. After the Rose Bowl win over Pacific-10 champion Washington, the streak stood at 22 quarters. The Huskies managed just two field goals on the day. Wolverine tailback Butch Woolfolk ran for 182 yards, including a six-yard touchdown run that put Michigan up 7–6 at halftime. Quarterback John Wangler and wide receiver Anthony Carter connected on a third-quarter touchdown pass. Michigan kicker Ali Haji-Sheikh added a 25-yard field goal and Don Bracken set a Rose Bowl record with a 73-yard punt. The 1–2 start to the season gave way to a nine-game winning streak and a No. 4 ranking in both polls.

Running back Butch Woolfolk romps through the Washington defense in Michigan's 1981 Rose Bowl win over the Huskies.

Jim Harbaugh, Jamie Morris and the Wolverines capped one of the most memorable seasons in UM history with a thrilling win over Nebraska.

1986 FIESTA BOWL
MICHIGAN 27, NEBRASKA 23

Michigan ended the 1985 regular season at 9–1–1 and boasted the nation's best scoring defense. Nebraska had won nine straight, sandwiched between losses in the opener and the finale. The two conference runners-up met in the Fiesta Bowl. A 42-yard field goal by Michigan's Pat Moons, set up by a 21-yard Jamie Morris run, was the extent of the scoring in the first quarter. Nebraska scored twice in the second period, on a short pass from McCathorn Clayton to Doug DuBose and a three-yard DuBose run, and the first half ended with the good guys trailing 14–3. But the Wolverines stormed back with 24 unanswered points in the third quarter, including a pair of short TD plunges by quarterback Jim Harbaugh, and held on for the win. Michigan forced six Cornhusker fumbles on the day, recovering three, and Dave Arnold blocked a punt to set up a short Moons field goal in the third period. With the win, Michigan finished the season ranked second nationally in both polls.

Jamie Morris

Demetrius Brown led a stirring 28–24 win over Alabama in the 1988 Hall of Fame Bowl.

1988 HALL OF FAME BOWL
MICHIGAN 28, ALABAMA 24

With Bo Schembechler recuperating from heart surgery, offensive coordinator Gary Moeller assumed coaching duties for the 1988 Hall of Fame Bowl against Alabama. On the game's opening possession, the Crimson Tide marched to the Michigan 34 and broke the ice with a 51-yard field goal. The Wolverines took control of the game in the second quarter with touchdown runs of 25 and 14 yards by Jamie Morris to take a 14–3 halftime lead. In the third period, Morris exploded for a 77-yard touchdown run, extending the margin to 21–3. But the Tide took the lead on 21 unanswered points. With a 16-yard pass from Jeff Dunn to Howard Cross and two Bobby Humphrey touchdown runs, Bama now led 24–21 with less than five minutes to go. With the clock winding down and Michigan facing fourth-and-three, quarterback Demetrius Brown hit flanker John Kolesar on a 20-yard touchdown strike for the 28–24 win. Morris ran for a Hall of Fame Bowl record and Michigan bowl-game record 234 yards.

Cornerback David Arnold (15) and the Wolverines gave Bo Schembechler a satisfying Rose Bowl win and a final fourth-place finish in the AP poll.

1989 ROSE BOWL
MICHIGAN 22, SOUTHERN CALIFORNIA 14

Bo Schembechler took his 11th-ranked Wolverines out to Pasadena to face once-beaten, fifth-ranked USC, led by Heisman Trophy runner-up Rodney Peete at quarterback, in the 1989 Rose Bowl. Michigan picked up where it had left off at the end of the previous season's Hall of Fame Bowl—with Demetrius Brown connecting with John Kolesar for 21 yards to set up a 49-yard Mike Gillette field goal. The first quarter ended 3–0 Michigan, but Peete scored twice on short runs in the second for a 14–3 SC lead at the half. That would close the book on the Trojans' scoring for the day. In the third, Brown scrambled 22 yards to the USC 6 then hit Chris Calloway on a six-yard scoring toss two plays later. A 23-yard Brown-to-Walker pass and a 61-yard Leroy Hoard run set up a pair of one-yard scoring plunges by Hoard in the fourth quarter. Linebacker John Milligan iced the victory with an interception of a Peete aerial with 50 seconds left. Hoard shredded the USC defense—the Pac-10's best that year—for 142 rushing yards on 19 carries. With the win, the Wolverines vaulted into fourth place in the final AP poll.

1991 GATOR BOWL
MICHIGAN 35, MISSISSIPPI 3

Gary Moeller's first Michigan team put the finishing touches on a 9–3 campaign with a 35–3 dismantling of Southeastern Conference runner-up Ole Miss in the Gator Bowl. The Rebels scored once, on a Gator Bowl record 51-yard field goal by Brian Lee in the second quarter. The Wolverines had opened the scoring in the first quarter on a 63-yard touchdown pass from Elvis Grbac to Desmond Howard and finished the rout with a 33-yard

Grbac-to-Derrick Alexander connection in the fourth. Howard found himself on the receiving end of two Grbac scoring tosses—the second came early in the third quarter and covered 50 yards. Two Wolverine running backs—Jon Vaughn and Ricky Powers—exceeded the 100-yard rushing mark. Michigan amassed 715 yards of total offense, and for their efforts offensive linemen Dean Dingman, Tom Dohring, Greg Skrepenak, Matt Elliott and Steve Everitt were named the game's Most Valuable Players.

1998 ROSE BOWL
MICHIGAN 21,
WASHINGTON STATE 16

Michigan added emphasis to its most recent national title with a 21–16 Rose Bowl victory over Pac-10 champion Washington State. A 15-yard scoring pass from Ryan Leaf to Kevin McKenzie put the Cougars on top 7–0 to end the first quarter. In the second, Michigan QB Brian Griese and wide receiver Tai Streets connected on the first of two long touchdown passes, from 53 yards out, to knot the score at 7 entering intermission. In the third period, Leaf engineered a 99-yard drive that culminated in a 14-yard reverse by wide receiver Michael Tims to reclaim the lead for the

Cougars. Michigan's James Hall blocked the PAT attempt and the score remained 13–7. Then came Griese-to-Streets II—a 58-yard scoring bomb that put the Wolverines up to stay, 14–13. In the fourth quarter, Griese found tight end Jerame Tuman from 23 yards out to extend the lead to 21–13. Washington State added a field goal to pull within striking distance at 21–16, but Michigan held the ball for the next seven minutes, converting three third downs in the process, and time ran out on the Cougars. Griese received game MVP honors on the strength of an 18-for-30, 251-yard, three touchdown passing performance. And the 12–0 Wolverines were national champions for the 11th time.

Mission accomplished: a tense 21–16 win over Washington State brought the Maize and Blue a long-awaited national championship.

1999 CITRUS BOWL
MICHIGAN 45, ARKANSAS 31

Michigan emerged victorious from its top-20 matchup with Arkansas in the 1999 Citrus Bowl. The Wolverines scored first on a 43-yard first-quarter field goal by Jay Feeley, but found themselves trailing 31–24 with 5:49 left to play. Coach Lloyd Carr's troops responded with 21 unanswered points in just 4:02 of playing time for the 45–31 win. A 21-yard touchdown pass from Tom Brady to DiAllo Johnson put the Wolverines ahead to stay. Anthony Thomas, Michigan's all-time leading rusher, ran for 139 yards and three touchdowns on that day and was awarded game MVP honors. Linebacker Sam Sword paced the Michigan defense with 11 tackles.

2000 ORANGE BOWL
MICHIGAN 35, ALABAMA 34

The Maize and Blue had to overcome 14-point deficits twice to score a 35–34 win over Alabama in the 2000 Orange Bowl, the first overtime game in Michigan history. Both teams entered the game with Top-10 national rankings. After a scoreless first quarter, the Crimson Tide took a 14–0 lead in the second on a pair of Shaun Alexander touchdown runs. The Wolverines answered with a 27-yard scoring pass from Tom Brady to David Terrell to close the gap to 14–7 at halftime, and a 57-yard Brady-to-Terrell strike in the third quarter knotted the score at 14. But the third-quarter fireworks had just started. Bama took another two-touchdown lead on a 50-yard Alexander run and a 62-yard Freddie Milons punt return, and Michigan pulled even with a 20-yard TD pass from Brady to Terrell and a three-yard Thomas touchdown run—all in the third quarter. A scoreless fourth period left the score tied 28-all after regulation. Brady hit tight end Shawn Thompson on a 25-yard scoring strike on Michigan's first play in overtime, and Hayden Epstein made what turned out to be the game-winning extra point. After Andrew Zow connected with Antonio Carter from 21 yards out to pull within one, Bama's PAT kick failed. Final score: Michigan 35, Alabama 34.

Wide receiver David Terrell stretches across the goal line for a third-quarter touchdown against Alabama in the 2000 Orange Bowl at Pro Player Stadium in Miami.

John Navarre and Chris Perry
dominated the 2003 Outback Bowl.

2003 OUTBACK BOWL
MICHIGAN 38, FLORIDA 30

Michigan quarterback John Navarre completed 21 of 36 pass attempts for 319 yards, and Florida's Rex Grossman went 21-of-41 for 323 yards. But it was the Chris Perry show. Michigan's junior running back ripped Florida's defense for 193 yards—85 rushing and 108 receiving—and scored four touchdowns in a 38–30 win over the Gators in the 2003 Outback Bowl. Perry's first score, a four-yard run, put the Maize and Blue up 7–0 in the first quarter. In the second, Earnest Graham gave the Gators a 13–7 lead on two touchdown runs, with a missed two-point try after the second. Michigan piled up the points, leading 21–16 at the half and 35–23 after three. Florida pulled within five on a three-yard scoring strike from Grossman to tight end Aaron Walker midway through the fourth period, then Michigan extended its lead to eight on a 33-yard Adam Finley field goal with 2:20 to play. Wolverine linebacker Victor Hobson sealed the 38–30 triumph with an interception of a wide receiver reverse pass with less than a minute to go and Florida driving.

— Greatest Games —

1950—MICHIGAN 9, OHIO STATE 3

It was more survival of the fittest than a game. Under the most trying of conditions, the Wolverines upset the Buckeyes in a game forever known as the "Snow Bowl." A two-day blizzard, including nine inches of snow the morning of the game, struck Columbus, Ohio, that weekend. Ice and snow covered the field and stands but amazingly, more than 50,000 spectators showed up for the annual classic. Michigan won despite not gaining a first down, failing to complete a pass and punting 24 times.

Late in the first half, Michigan's Tony Momsen blocked a Vic Janowicz punt and recovered it in the end zone for a touchdown. Neither team scored in the second half, and Michigan, which entered the game with a 4–3–1 record, wound up with a Rose Bowl berth.

24 punts, zero first downs—and a 9-3 win over Ohio State. The "Snow Bowl" win put Michigan in the Rose Bowl.

Barry Pierson's 60-yard punt return set up Michigan's decisive touchdown in one of Bo Schembechler's greatest wins.

1969—MICHIGAN 24, OHIO STATE 12

Woody and Bo. Bo and Woody. This is where an already steaming rivalry turned white-hot as first-year Michigan coach Bo Schembechler guided the Wolverines to a stunning upset of the top-ranked Buckeyes, who had won 22 straight games and seemed destined to repeat as national champions.

Still fuming over a 36-point loss in Columbus the previous season in which Woody Hayes ran up the score, the fired-up Wolverines forced seven turnovers and held the Buckeyes scoreless in the second half. Michigan fullback Garvie Craw scored two rushing touchdowns.

1995—MICHIGAN 31, OHIO STATE 23

Tshimanga Biakabutuka spoke five languages fluently but his thundering feet did all the talking on this afternoon. Biakabutuka rushed for 313 yards as the Wolverines upset the second-ranked Buckeyes. Biakabutuka gained 22 yards on his first carry and continued to gouge the Ohio State defense, upstaging Ohio State Heisman winner Eddie George in the process.

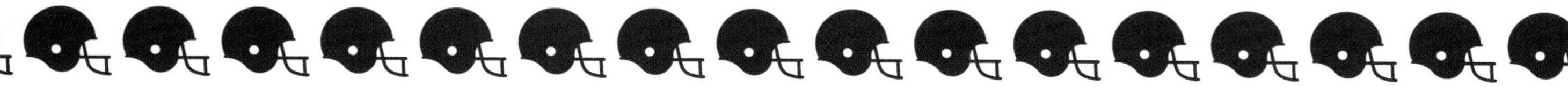

1997—MICHIGAN 20, OHIO STATE 14

A perfect regular season, a victory over their hated rival, a trip to the Rose Bowl and a Heisman-clinching performance. It was all of those things rolled into one sweet, if tense, afternoon for Michigan fans as the Wolverines had many reasons to celebrate. Junior defensive back Charles Woodson won over a majority of Heisman Trophy voters with a 78-yard punt return for a touchdown and a crucial interception. The top-ranked Wolverines maintained their unbeaten season but it wasn't easy. After Michigan built a 20–0 lead, the Buckeyes cut the deficit to six with the aid of a fumble by Wolverines quarterback Brian Griese inside his own 10-yard line. Linebacker Ian Gold batted down a fourth-down pass attempt to secure the win. The Wolverines went on to win their first national championship in 49 years, beating Washington State in the Rose Bowl.

Michigan quarterback Brian Griese reacts to the crowd after the Wolverines' 20–14 victory over Ohio State in 1997, earning top-ranked Michigan a trip to the Rose Bowl.

2001—MICHIGAN STATE 26, MICHIGAN 24

It came down to the last second, even if Michigan followers will go to their graves believing the Spartans undeservingly got an extra play. Michigan came into the game with a 4–0 Big Ten record and left in anger and disbelief. The Wolverines thought they had stopped MSU at the Michigan 2-yard line but somehow the clock read 0:01 when MSU Jeff Smoker intentionally spiked the ball. Given one last chance, Smoker threw a 2-yard touchdown pass to running back T.J. Duckett to give the Spartans the victory and ensure a ceaseless controversy.

Michigan State's final drive was prolonged by two Michigan penalties, including a personal foul call on a fourth-down pass. A 20-yard touchdown pass from John Navarre to Jermaine Gonzales put the Wolverines in front earlier in the fourth quarter.

2003—MICHIGAN 38, MINNESOTA 35

Even the Wolverines had a hard time fathoming how they erased a 21-point, fourth-quarter deficit and salvaged their season in Minnesota's Metrodome. "We still don't know what happened," defensive end Larry Stevens said after Michigan scored 31 points in the final quarter to produce the biggest comeback in school history.

Quarterback John Navarre passed for 353 yards, all but 50 after halftime. He threw two fourth-quarter touchdown passes and caught another from receiver Steve Breaston. Running back Chris Perry caught 11 passes for 122 yards and rushed for another 84 yards. Freshman placekicker Garrett Rivas made a 33-yard field goal with 47 seconds left to complete the rally.

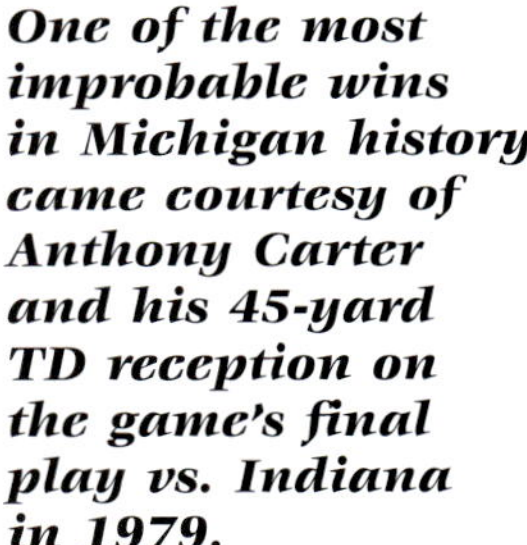

One of the most improbable wins in Michigan history came courtesy of Anthony Carter and his 45-yard TD reception on the game's final play vs. Indiana in 1979.

Classic Moments

1940—MICHIGAN 40, OHIO STATE 0

The thought is almost unfathomable: Ohio State fans giving a Wolverines player a standing ovation. But Tom Harmon, Michigan's first Heisman Trophy winner, was so dominant that the people of Columbus could only stand and applaud. Harmon ran for 139 yards and two touchdowns, completed 11 of 12 passes for 151 yards and two touchdowns, intercepted three passes and kicked four extra points.

1979—MICHIGAN 27, INDIANA 21

With six seconds left and the Wolverines on the Hoosiers' 45-yard line, it appeared the game would end in a tie. Freshman wide receiver Anthony Carter would not allow that to happen. Carter told quarterback John Wangler to throw the ball to him. Wangler complied and Carter did the rest. Nearly slipping to the ground after he caught the ball, Carter cut and spun around defenders until he high-stepped into the end zone.

It was a game that defined a career: Desmond Howard stretches for the clinching touchdown vs. Notre Dame (above) on a daring fourth-and inches play, after another TD earlier in the 24–14 win (right).

1991—MICHIGAN 24, NOTRE DAME 14

Elvis Grbac's pass was about to bounce harmlessly to the ground when suddenly, wide receiver Desmond Howard swooped in like a seagull. Howard dove, stretched out his arms as far as possible, and caught the football. The fourth-down touchdown pass with the Wolverines leading by three at the time clinched a Michigan victory in a matchup of top 10 teams. The play sparked Howard's Heisman Trophy season.

1994—COLORADO 27, MICHIGAN 26

The Wolverines have suffered an occasional heartbreaking loss at Michigan Stadium but nothing came as a bigger shock than this one. On the game's final play, Colorado quarterback Kordell Stewart heaved a 64-yard touchdown pass to Michael Westbrook to give the Buffaloes an improbable victory. Backup wide receiver Blake Anderson tipped the ball and Westbrook grabbed the carom as 106,427 fans watched in stunned disbelief.

1997—MICHIGAN 23, MICHIGAN STATE 7

Defensive back Charles Woodson made many eye-popping plays while winning the Heisman Trophy that season. None was more spectacular than his leaping, one-handed interception along the sidelines against the Spartans. On a pass that was being intentionally thrown out of bounds, Woodson grabbed the ball, twisted his body and landed with one foot inbounds.

THE RIVALRIES

Some great rivalries have helped define Michigan football and have given fans many of their greatest memories. One of those rivalries just might be the greatest in all of sports.

Michigan vs. Ohio State

They may develop it during childhood. They may develop it as a recruit. They may develop it the moment they walk in as freshmen.

Every self-respecting University of Michigan football player gains a healthy dislike for anything Scarlet & Gray. It's a time-honored tradition that spans more than a century and fosters what many consider the greatest rivalry in sports.

A Michigan–Ohio State football game is a "must-see" spectacle every November and carries special meaning to every player, coach and fan, regardless of what the teams' record may be in any given season.

Michigan and Ohio State played their first game in 1897, a 34–0 Wolverines victory. The game has been played every season since 1918, a streak that ranks 10th in NCAA Division I-A for longest uninterrupted series. Since 1922, more fans have attended the game than any other college football matchup.

In the early stages, Michigan dominated the series. The Wolverines were 13–0–2 in the first 15 meetings, including a humiliating 86–0 blowout in 1902. Ohio State finally broke through in 1919 with a 13–3 victory.

From that point, the annual border war began to heat up. Though the teams do not play for a trophy, there are usually bigger prizes at stake.

Since the game was moved to the final Saturday of the Big Ten season in 1935, it has impacted the conference title race 42 times. On 20 occasions, the teams have decided the Big Ten championship amongst themselves.

"Any time you play in this game, it's exciting," Michigan coach Lloyd Carr said. "When the championship is on the line, I don't think it gets much better than that."

Michigan leads the series 57–39–6 but that edge shrinks to 45–39–4 since 1918. Neither team has won more than four straight since 1927, though the upper hand has shifted back and forth through the years.

In 1922, the Wolverines spoiled Ohio Stadium's dedication game with a 19–0 triumph. Harry Kipke was the star, scoring two touchdowns and kicking a field goal. In the series' first game at newly constructed Michigan Stadium in 1927, the Wolverines once again posted a shutout victory, 21–0.

Ohio State controlled the series from 1934–37, shutting out the Wolverines four

consecutive times. Michigan responded with three consecutive victories of its own, including Heisman Trophy winner Tom Harmon's amazing 1940 performance. He ran and passed for four touchdowns and returned an interception for another in a 40–0 Wolverines romp.

Michigan had a 6–0–1 record from 1945–51, including the unforgettable "Snow Bowl." The 1950 game in Columbus was played under conditions that only a penguin could love. The state of Ohio was buried under a foot of snow, and it blew so hard around Ohio Stadium it was almost impossible to see. The field was completely obliterated. Nobody had any idea where the yard lines were. There were several inches of snow on the ground, piles of snow stacked around the field and more coming down every minute. The temperature registered near zero and the wind was blowing through the stadium at 28 miles an hour. Minus-29 degree wind chill. The teams would run a play and then the sweepers would race on the field to see where the ball was resting. They sold almost 80,000 tickets for the game and, amazingly, 50,503 showed up in those miserable conditions. Michigan won 9–3 without making a first down, completing a pass or having a run of over six yards. The Wolverines' points came on a safety and a touchdown off blocked punts. The win secured coach Bennie Oosterbaan's Michigan team its fourth straight Big Ten title.

The Buckeyes, heading toward a national championship, drove 99 yards for the go-ahead touchdown in a 21–7 win in 1954. Ohio State dominated the classic from 1954–68, winning 11 of 15 meetings.

Then came what many consider the most important and greatest non-bowl victory in Wolverines history. Under the guidance of first-year coach and former Woody Hayes assistant Bo Schembechler, Michigan shocked the top-ranked Buckeyes 24–12 in Michigan Stadium and snapped Ohio State's 22-game winning streak in 1969.

Hayes called that Ohio State club the best he ever coached. The Buckeyes had defeated all of their previous opponents by 27 or more points. But Michigan players were still steaming from Hayes' decision to go for two points late in Ohio State's 50–14 romp the previous season, and Schembechler made the Wolverines believe they could pull off the upset. Michigan scored all of its points in the first half, then held the Buckeyes scoreless in the second.

At a banquet honoring the 1969 Wolverines team, Hayes let his protege know how he felt.

"Damn you, Bo," Hayes growled. "You will never win a bigger game than that."

The game's implications regularly impacted the national landscape during the Schembechler era. From 1972–81, every Michigan–Ohio State game determined who would represent the conference in the Rose Bowl.

Ironically, a tie produced one of the bitterest memories in Wolverines' football history. Michigan believed it was headed to the Rose Bowl after rallying to tie the Buckeyes 10–10 in the 1973 game. A committee of Big Ten athletic directors chose Ohio State as the league's Rose Bowl representative because of an injury suffered by Michigan quarterback Dennis Franklin during the game.

The 1974 and '75 games, both Buckeyes victories, showcased two-time Heisman Trophy

winner Archie Griffin. Hayes coached his last game against Michigan in 1978, a 14–3 Wolverines win.

Wolverines quarterback Jim Harbaugh issued "The Guarantee" in 1986. After Minnesota dashed Michigan's hopes of an undefeated season the previous week, Harbaugh guaranteed the Wolverines would beat their fiercest rival. They did, but Michigan needed a missed 45-yard field goal try by Ohio State's Matt Franz to clinch the 26–24 victory.

From 1988 to 2000, Michigan had a 10–2–1 record against the Buckeyes and Ohio State coach John Cooper.

"My record against Michigan speaks for itself," Cooper said.

The most memorable play during that era was Desmond Howard's 93-yard punt return in 1991 for a touchdown. Upon reaching the end zone, Howard struck his famed Heisman pose. Howard won the award the following month.

In 1997 with Carr as head coach, the top-ranked Wolverines defeated the fourth-ranked Buckeyes 20–14 to gain a Rose Bowl berth. Defensive back Charles Woodson's 78-yard

punt return was the pivotal play in the game and propelled him to a Heisman Trophy.

"Charles Woodson certainly played one of his greatest games in the very, very biggest game we have at Michigan, in a game that meant everything to us," Lloyd Carr said.

Michigan went on to win a share of the national championship by defeating Washington State in the Rose Bowl.

The 2003 game marked the 100th game in the storied rivalry. The Wolverines prevailed 35–21 and headed to the Rose Bowl for the first time since the undefeated 1997 season. The game was witnessed by a NCAA record-breaking 112,118 fans at Michigan Stadium.

"We've tasted greatness but we never got it," Michigan senior running back Chris Perry said. "We never really succeeded in accomplishing something great. But we did it today."

That, however, was Michigan's only victory from 2001 to 2005 as momentum shifted back to the Buckeyes under coach Jim Tressel. Ohio State's tense 14–9 win in 2002 was a springboard to a Buckeyes' national championship.

Michigan vs. Notre Dame

Here's a little-known item of football trivia: Michigan taught Notre Dame how to play football. The first three football games Notre Dame ever played were against Michigan — one in 1887 and two in 1888 — and Michigan won all three.

No college football programs have enjoyed more success than Michigan and Notre Dame. Michigan ranks No. 1 in all-time victories; the Fighting Irish are second. Notre Dame has won 12 national championships, tops among Division I-A schools; the Wolverines claim 11. Many would also rate their respective fight songs as the finest in the land.

Put these two teams together on the same field and they're bound to produce pulsating, dramatic games filled with lasting memories.

Michigan's football history with Notre Dame goes back even longer than its rivalry with Ohio State. In fact, the Fighting Irish played the first game in their storied history against the Wolverines. Michigan scored two touchdowns, then worth four points, in a 30-minute game played on a muddy field for an 8–0 victory.

A bitter feud between the schools, mainly between Michigan coach Fielding Yost and Notre Dame's Knute Rockne, resulted in an

All-America DB Garland Rivers skies for an interception attempt vs. Notre Dame.

interruption in the series from 1909 to 1942. After two war-time games, Michigan coach Fritz Crisler decided to take the Irish off the schedule once again.

The teams did not play again for 35 years. After Crisler retired in 1968, new Wolverines athletic director Don Canham approached Notre Dame's executive vice president, Rev. Edmund Joyce, about resuming the series. Scheduling conflicts prevented that from happening until 1978.

It was worth the wait. Except for three two-year breaks, the teams have played annually ever since that resumption. Usually played early in the season, the rivalry game brings out the best in both schools and often foreshadows the kind of season each team will have.

Quarterback Rick Leach overcame a sprained ankle to lead Michigan to a 28–14 victory in the much-anticipated 1978 matchup. A majority of the games since then have been in doubt right to the finish. In the last 21 meetings, 14 have been decided by seven points or less.

In 1980, Michigan scored a touchdown in the final minute but Notre Dame prevailed 29–27 on a last-second, 51-yard field goal by Harry Oliver.

"I hated to lose that game in the worst way," Wolverines coach Bo Schembechler said.

"It was the type of game you win 20 times and lose 21 times."

Schembechler's team got its revenge the following season, beating the No. 1–ranked Irish 25–7.

Michigan spoiled Lou Holtz's Notre Dame head coaching debut in 1986 with a 24–23 victory but lost the next four years to the Irish. Notre Dame receiver Raghib (Rocket) Ismail was the star in the 1989 matchup when the teams were ranked first and second in the polls. Ismail returned two kickoffs for second-half touchdowns in the 24–19 Irish win.

That agonizing stretch in Wolverines history ended with the outstretched arms of Desmond Howard. In 1991, Howard made what is generally considered the greatest touchdown catch in Michigan history.

With the Wolverines leading 17–14, Michigan was faced with a fourth down at the

Notre Dame 25-yard-line. Needing a foot to gain a first down, quarterback Elvis Grbac lofted a post pass that seemed out of Howard's reach. Fully extended, Howard made a diving grab in the right corner of the end zone to secure a 24–14 victory.

The 1994 game produced another classic. Notre Dame took the lead 24–23 with 52 seconds remaining when Derrick Mayes caught a 7-yard touchdown pass from quarterback Ron Powlus. Michigan quarterback Todd Collins responded with a scoring drive that culminated with a 42-yard Remy Hamilton field goal with two seconds left, giving Michigan a 26–24 victory.

The most lopsided game of the series occurred in 2003, when Michigan rolled to a 38–0 victory. Through 2005, Michigan leads the series 18–14–1.

—— Michigan vs. Michigan State ——

Some rivalries divide states. Others turn cities, offices and families against each other.

Once every year, the state splits up between Michigan's Maize and Blue and Michigan State's Green and White when the two schools meet on the football field. Their colors clearly don't mix.

Wolverines fans view the Spartans as annoying neighbors. MSU supporters feel Michigan fans act high and mighty and look down upon them.

Their football teams first crossed paths in 1898, when MSU was called Michigan Agricultural College. The Aggies didn't put up much of a fight in the first three meetings, losing by a combined score of 204–0.

Michigan held their in-state competitors scoreless in 20 of the first 27 meetings, until Michigan State responded with four consecutive wins from 1934–37. Michigan won the next 10 meetings but MSU dominated the series during the decades of the '50s and '60s, going 14–4–2 during that span.

Since 1953 when Michigan State began Big Ten play, the rivals have gotten something more than bragging rights. The victor lays claim to the four-foot, wooden Paul Bunyan Trophy, which was donated to the schools by Michigan Governor G. Mennen Williams.

The trophy displays the legendary Bunyan with his feet planted on a map of the state and an axe lying near his left foot. A Michigan State flag rests above Bunyan's right foot and a University of Michigan flag hangs above his left foot.

Beginning in 1970, Bo Schembechler's second season as Michigan's head coach, the Wolverines have dominated their in-state rival. The Wolverines, who hold a 65–28–5 advantage in the series, have won 28 of the last 36 meetings against the Spartans and MSU has failed to win in back-to-back seasons.

The schools have staged some epic and sometimes controversial duels over the past two decades. Wolverines fans lament the 1990 and 2001 games when the Spartans won tight games with unusual endings.

Ranked No. 1 entering the 1990 matchup, Michigan went for a two-point conversion during the closing moments to win the game. Receiver Desmond Howard was tripped up by defensive back Eddie Brown while trying to catch a go-ahead pass but no penalty was called. The upset by the unranked Spartans helped them gain a share of the Big Ten title with the Wolverines.

Michigan State's clock operator was in the eye of the storm 11 years later at Spartan Stadium. With MSU trailing 24–20, the Wolverines defense appeared to have stopped the Spartans two yards shy of the goal line. With Michigan State out of timeouts, quarterback Jeff Smoker spiked the ball and 0:01 still appeared on the game clock. While Michigan players and coaches screamed that the clock was stopped prematurely, the Spartans huddled up for one more play. Smoker threw a touchdown pass to running back T.J. Duckett and Michigan left the premises with steam coming out of their ears.

"It's a rivalry where the two schools don't like each other," then-MSU coach Bobby Williams said. "It's everything. It's the fans, the players, the coaches, you name it. They have that game marked; we have that game marked."

Three seasons later with John L. Smith coaching the Spartans and Lloyd Carr on the Michigan sidelines, MSU left Michigan Stadium in a state of shock and disbelief. In an epic battle that required three overtimes to decide, the Wolverines squeaked out a thrilling 45–37 victory.

MSU had a 27–10 lead with less than seven minutes left. The Wolverines then staged an amazing comeback to tie the game. Wide receiver Braylon Edwards made two leaping grabs in the end zone, hauling in the touchdown passes from freshman quarterback Chad Henne, to even the score at 27–27.

After the teams traded field goals in the first overtime session and touchdowns in the second OT, Michigan moved ahead on another Henne-to-Edwards scoring pass and a two-point conversion. The Wolverines' defense stopped the Spartans on their final possession to secure the victory.

"I think this game speaks to the spirit of the stadium, to the tradition and this rivalry," Carr said afterward. "Anybody who saw this game either in this stadium or across the country on television saw one of the greatest football games, in my opinion, ever played."

There's surely more drama to come, especially when the schools play their 100th game in 2007.

Michigan vs. Minnesota

When Michigan plays Minnesota, the reward is one of the oddest and oldest trophies in college football. The Little Brown Jug is handed to the winner and has more than a century of history behind it.

Michigan team manager Tommy Roberts originally purchased the jug, which weighs nearly 15 pounds and can hold approximately five gallons of water, from a Minneapolis store in 1903 for 30 cents. Roberts bought the jug because head coach Fielding Yost anticipated that Minnesota would not provide the Michigan players with pure water.

The Golden Gophers entered the 1903 game unbeaten that season, and the Wolverines were riding a 28-game winning streak. The game ended prematurely in a 6–6 tie as spectators rushed the field. In Michigan's haste to leave the field, the Wolverines left the jug behind.

Minnesota's equipment manager, Oscar Munson, found the jug the following day and gave it to the school's athletic director, L.J. Cooke. Inspired by the team's effort, Cooke had the jug inscribed "Michigan Jug—Captured by Oscar, October 31, 1903."

Yost wrote a letter to Cooke, asking him to return the jug. Cooke responded, "If you want it, you'll have to come up and win it."

The oldest trophy game in college football was born, but the Wolverines had to wait until 1909 to get back the coveted prize because the

schools didn't play again until that season. Michigan finally recaptured the jug with a 15–6 victory.

In 1930, the jug was stolen from the Michigan athletic department and couldn't be found for four years, until an Ann Arbor gas station attendant discovered it behind some bushes. Now stored in a metal case, the Jug is painted in the colors of each school and features the score of each game.

In most years, the Jug can be found at the Wolverines' football offices. The Wolverines have dominated the series with a 67–24–3 record.

Minnesota won nine straight meetings from 1934 to 1942 and posted four consecutive victories from 1960-63. Minnesota's 7–6 win in

1940 had the greatest implications, since the Gophers were ranked No. 2 nationally, one spot ahead of the Wolverines.

Otherwise, the rivalry has been a lopsided one since the schools began playing annually in 1929. Michigan had a seven-game winning streak from 1943 to 1949, a nine-game streak from 1968 to 1976, an eight-game streak from 1978 to 1985 and a 16-game streak from 1987 to 2004.

The most exciting finish occurred in 2003, when the Wolverines rallied from a 21-point deficit in the final quarter to beat the Gophers 38–35 at Minnesota's Metrodome. The Golden Gophers finally ended the Wolverines' latest streak with a 23–20 victory at Michigan Stadium in 2005.

The Little Brown Jug

TALKIN' MICHIGAN FOOTBALL

We thought we'd go straight to the source and let some of Michigan's greatest legends share their thoughts about Wolverine football.

"It was a great experience. It's just a great feeling.
Nothing that happens now will take away from what we did as a team. We played the toughest schedule and went 12–0. We feel we're the best team in the country right now." —JON JANSEN, MICHIGAN OFFENSIVE TACKLE, AFTER THE WOLVERINES' 21–16 WIN OVER WASHINGTON STATE IN THE ROSE BOWL GAVE MICHIGAN THE 1997 NATIONAL CHAMPIONSHIP

"These are the types of games when championships are won. We've got to go in there and take their stadium over." —SAM SWORD, LINEBACKER, PRIOR TO THE 1997 PENN STATE GAME, WON BY MICHIGAN 34–8 IN HAPPY VALLEY

"This is as good a defense as I've seen since I've been here. And it may be the best." —BO SCHEMBECHLER, U-M LEGEND, ON THE 1997 CHAMPIONSHIP DEFENSE

"We didn't use a single substitute. After the game, we were enjoying ourselves in the hotel lobby when (Coach Fielding) Yost suddenly became aware that our three substitutes were missing. He asked Dan McGugin, our left guard (and longtime Vanderbilt coach), and me to look them up. We found them in back turning a garden hose on each other and rolling in the dirt—in full uniform. They told us they were ashamed to go home and have it known they hadn't gotten in the game." —MICHIGAN IMMORTAL WILLIE HESTON, ON THE FIRST ROSE BOWL GAME, WON BY MICHIGAN 49–0 OVER STANFORD

"Forty-six years and them bums ain't improved a lick." —AN ONLOOKER OBSERVING THAT MICHIGAN WON ITS FIRST TWO ROSE BOWL APPEARANCES, IN 1902 AND 1948, BY IDENTICAL 49–0 SCORES

"Michigan showed such a superlative poise and versatility in every department, such a wealth of offensive weapons and the talent to use them that it seemed a sacrilege to mention any other college team in the same breath." —LEGENDARY SPORTSWRITER RED SMITH ON MICHIGAN'S 1947 TEAM, WHICH WAS CROWNED NATIONAL CHAMPION IN A SPECIAL VOTE TAKEN AFTER THE BOWL GAMES. MICHIGAN TROUNCED SOUTHERN CAL 49–0 IN THE ROSE BOWL, WHILE REGULAR-SEASON NATIONAL CHAMPION NOTRE DAME HAD BEATEN THE TROJANS 38–7.

"Taylor's to the 20, down to the 15, down to the 10, the 5. Four, three, two, one. Touchdown Billy Taylor! Touchdown Billy Taylor! Billy Taylor scored a touchdown from 21 yards out! Old man Ufer's been broadcasting for 27 years, and I have never seen anything like this! Oh. Oh my eyes! I'm an old man. I've got maize and blue spots in front of me right now." —BOB UFER'S LEGENDARY CALL OF THE WINNING TOUCHDOWN IN MICHIGAN'S 10–7 WIN OVER OHIO STATE IN 1971

GO BL
M CLUB SUPPC

"Even though the game has changed, there is a connection between all of the players and coaches though the years. Once you are a Wolverine, you are always a Wolverine." —RON KRAMER, END 1954–56

"Bo is to Michigan what macaroni is to cheese. He means more to the state than any particular individual, and it's obvious from walking through campus that his leaving has had a tremendous impact at a time when students should be studying for finals." —MICHIGAN STUDENT ADAM SCHRAGER, ON THE OCCASION OF BO SCHEMBECHLER'S RETIREMENT

"When I make it to a game, I still get a thrill when the band comes out and plays the fight song. Chills still go up and down my spine when the players emerge from the tunnel and jump to touch the M banner. Even though I'm watching the game and not on the field, I still have great pride for Michigan football. It's something you never lose." —JACK WEISENBURGER, FULLBACK 1944–47

"From a social standpoint, it was very important. It made me feel proud that my teammates, black and white, truly believed there was no difference between us." —RON JOHNSON, HALFBACK 1965–68 ON BEING THE SCHOOL'S FIRST AFRICAN-AMERICAN CAPTAIN

"You had to be a real man to get out of the Michigan locker room that day. Players were pushing to get out of the door. When we took the field, no one felt their feet touch the ground." —BILLY TAYLOR, TAILBACK 1969–71, ON THE 24–12 UPSET OF OHIO STATE IN 1969

"There is a special breed of people that play at Michigan. They are goal-oriented, they want the very best. They want a great education, to play on a championship team and to do things right." —LES MILES, GUARD 1974–75

"Hey, Woody, maybe you know now, we're Michigan. We're not 'That team up north! We're Michigan!'"* —RICK LEACH, QUARTERBACK 1975–78 ON WHAT HE SAID TO OHIO STATE COACH WOODY HAYES AFTER MICHIGAN'S 14–3 WIN OVER THE BUCKEYES IN 1978

"What it means to be a Wolverine is being a part of the great history of Michigan. It's about the memories, friendships and the accomplishments of the team. Being in the huddle, looking at the faces of those guys you played with and trying to get the job done. There's always that excitement and freshness to Michigan football."* —HARLAN HUCKLEBY, TAILBACK 1975–78

"If Michigan teaches anything, it is that it takes a team to win. The mystique, tradition and everything associated with Michigan Wolverine football all revolves around the concept of a team. It isn't about individual accomplishments. It is learning to appreciate the value of a team, seeing teammates lay it all out on the line for the betterment of the team."* —BUTCH WOOLFOLK, TAILBACK 1978–81

One of the greatest athletes in Michigan history, Rick Leach was the All–Big Ten quarterback three times in his remarkable career.

Jamie Morris ran wild against Ohio State, shredding the Buckeyes for 210 yards in 1986 and 130 yards in 1987.

"A Michigan Wolverine is a man with dignity and a man with pride. If you give it your all at Michigan, you get everything out of it. As you're taught when you're younger, you always need to seize the opportunity. Being a Wolverine is being that man who seizes the moment." **—MERCURY HAYES, WIDE RECEIVER 1992–95**

"What stands out for me is when I stood out there on that podium at the Rose Bowl and the trophy was presented. I can remember looking out at that stadium and knowing that we had just won the national championship. A bunch of guys had taken a lot of criticism and we knew that together we had done something historic. I've had plenty of special moments at Michigan, but that stands out." **—COACH LLOYD CARR, 1995–PRESENT, ON WINNING THE 1997 NATIONAL CHAMPIONSHIP**

Anthony Carter evades Notre Dame defender Jim Stone during the 1980 Michigan–ND thriller.

FACTS AND FIGURES

— Michigan —
in the College Football Hall of Fame

COACHES		
NAME	YEARS	INDUCTED
Fritz Crisler	1937–1947	1954
George Little	1922–1924	1955
Glen E. "Bo" Schembechler	1969–1989	1993
Elton "Tad" Wieman	1921–1928	1956
Fielding Yost	1901–1924, 1926	1951

PLAYERS

NAME	POSITION	YEARS	INDUCTED
Albert Benbrook	Guard	1908–1910	1971
Anthony Carter	Wide Receiver	1979–1982	2001
Bob Chappuis	Halfback	1942, 46–47	1988
Dan Dierdorf	Tackle	1968–1970	2000
Chalmers "Bump" Elliott	Halfback	1946–1947	1989
Pete Elliott	Quarterback	1945–1948	1994
Bennie Friedman	Quarterback	1923–1926	1951
Tom Harmon	Halfback	1938–1940	1954
Willie Heston	Halfback	1901–1904	1954
Elroy Hirsch	Halfback	1943	1974
Ron Johnson	Halfback	1966–1968	1992
Harry Kipke	Halfback	1920–1923	1958
Ron Kramer	End	1953–1956	1978
John Maulbetsch	Halfback	1914–1916	1973
Reggie McKenzie	Guard	1969–1971	2002
Harry Newman	Quarterback	1931–1933	1954
Bennie Oosterbaan	End	1924–1927	1954
Merv Pregulman	Guard/Tackle	1940–1943	1982
Adolph "Germany" Schultz	Center	1904–1908	1951
Neil Snow	End/Fullback	1898–1901	1960
Ernie Vick	Center	1917–1921	1983
Bob Westfall	Fullback	1938–1941	1987
Albert Wistert	Tackle	1938–1942	1968
Alvin Wistert	Tackle	1946–1949	1981
Francis Wistert	Tackle	1930–1933	1967

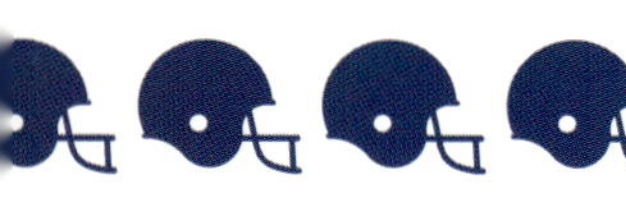

In 1947, Bob Chappuis (with the ball) accounted for 1,674 yards of total offense for the unbeaten Wolverines.

Bowl Game Results

RECORD: 18-19

1902 Rose Bowl	Michigan 49, Stanford 0
1948 Rose Bowl	Michigan 49, Southern California 0
1951 Rose Bowl	Michigan 14, California 6
1965 Rose Bowl	Michigan 34, Oregon State 7
1970 Rose Bowl	Southern California 10, Michigan 3
1972 Rose Bowl	Stanford 13, Michigan 12
1976 Orange Bowl	Oklahoma 14, Michigan 6
1977 Rose Bowl	Southern California 14, Michigan 6
1978 Rose Bowl	Washington 27, Michigan 20
1979 Rose Bowl	Southern California 17, Michigan 10
1979 Gator Bowl	North Carolina 17, Michigan 15

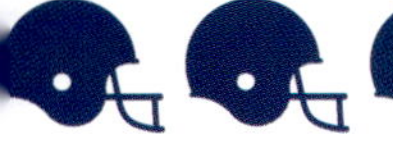

1981 Rose Bowl	Michigan 23, Washington 6
1981 Bluebonnet Bowl	Michigan 33, UCLA 14
1983 Rose Bowl	UCLA 24, Michigan 14
1984 Sugar Bowl	Auburn 9, Michigan 7
1984 Holiday Bowl	BYU 24, Michigan 17
1986 Fiesta Bowl	Michigan 27, Nebraska 23
1987 Rose Bowl	Arizona State 22, Michigan 15
1988 Hall of Fame Bowl	Michigan 28, Alabama 24
1989 Rose Bowl	Michigan 22, Southern California 14
1990 Rose Bowl	Southern California 17, Michigan 10
1991 Gator Bowl	Michigan 35, Mississippi 3
1992 Rose Bowl	Washington 34, Michigan 14
1993 Rose Bowl	Michigan 38, Washington 31
1994 Hall of Fame Bowl	Michigan 42, NC State 7
1994 Holiday Bowl	Michigan 24, Colorado State 14
1995 Alamo Bowl	Texas A&M 22, Michigan 20
1997 Outback Bowl	Alabama 17, Michigan 14
1998 Rose Bowl	Michigan 21, Washington State 16
1999 Citrus Bowl	Michigan 45, Arkansas 31
2000 Orange Bowl	Michigan 35, Alabama 34
2001 Citrus Bowl	Michigan 31, Auburn 28
2002 Citrus Bowl	Tennessee 45, Michigan 17
2003 Outback Bowl	Michigan 38, Florida 30
2004 Rose Bowl	USC 28, Michigan 14
2005 Rose Bowl	Texas 38, Michigan 37
2005 Alamo Bowl	Nebraska 32, Michigan 28

Michigan's Consensus All-Americans

YEAR	PLAYER, POSITION
1898	William Cunningham, C
1901	Neil Snow, E
1903	Willie Heston, B
1904	Willie Heston, B
1907	Adolph Schultz, C
1909	Albert Benbrook, G
1910	Stanfield Wells, E; Albert Benbrook, G
1913	Miller Pontius, T; Jim Craig, B
1914	John Maulbetsch, B
1922	Harry Kipke, B
1923	Jack Blott, C

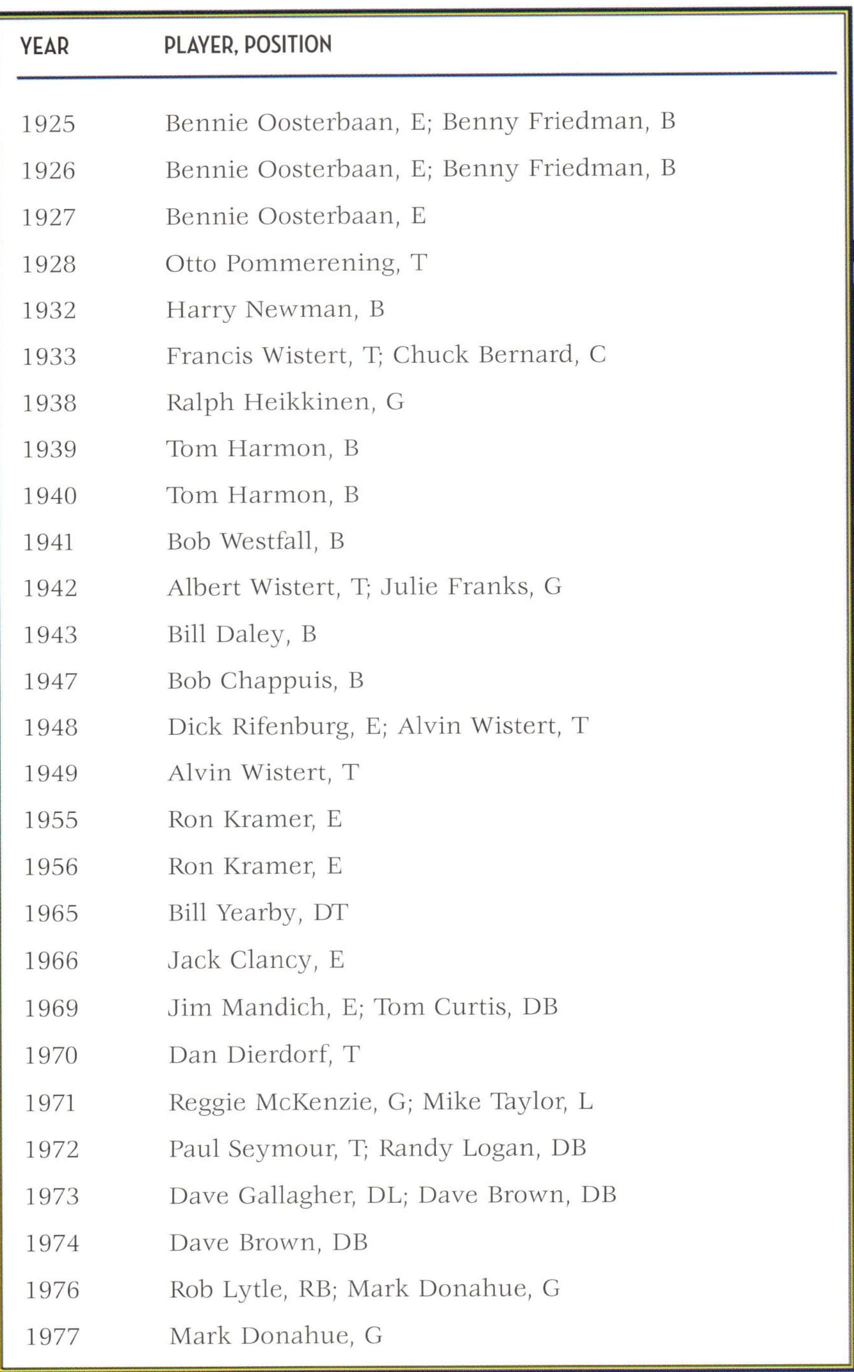

YEAR	PLAYER, POSITION
1925	Bennie Oosterbaan, E; Benny Friedman, B
1926	Bennie Oosterbaan, E; Benny Friedman, B
1927	Bennie Oosterbaan, E
1928	Otto Pommerening, T
1932	Harry Newman, B
1933	Francis Wistert, T; Chuck Bernard, C
1938	Ralph Heikkinen, G
1939	Tom Harmon, B
1940	Tom Harmon, B
1941	Bob Westfall, B
1942	Albert Wistert, T; Julie Franks, G
1943	Bill Daley, B
1947	Bob Chappuis, B
1948	Dick Rifenburg, E; Alvin Wistert, T
1949	Alvin Wistert, T
1955	Ron Kramer, E
1956	Ron Kramer, E
1965	Bill Yearby, DT
1966	Jack Clancy, E
1969	Jim Mandich, E; Tom Curtis, DB
1970	Dan Dierdorf, T
1971	Reggie McKenzie, G; Mike Taylor, L
1972	Paul Seymour, T; Randy Logan, DB
1973	Dave Gallagher, DL; Dave Brown, DB
1974	Dave Brown, DB
1976	Rob Lytle, RB; Mark Donahue, G
1977	Mark Donahue, G

YEAR	PLAYER, POSITION
1979	Ron Simpkins, LB
1981	Anthony Carter, WR; Ed Muransky, OL; Kurt Becker, OL
1982	Anthony Carter, WR
1985	Mike Hammerstein, DL; Brad Cochran, DB
1986	Garland Rivers, DB
1987	John Elliot, OL
1988	John Vitale, C; Mark Messner, DL
1989	Tripp Welborne, DB
1990	Tripp Welborne, DB
1991	Desmond Howard, WR; Greg Skrepenak, OL
1996	Jarrett Irons, LB
1997	Charles Woodson, DB
2000	Steve Hutchinson, OL
2003	Chris Perry, RB
2004	Braylon Edwards, WR; David Baas, OL; Marlin Jackson, DB; Ernest Shazor, DB

Career Statistical Leaders

Tyrone Wheatley amassed 20 100-yard rushing games during his Michigan career.

Rushes: 924, Anthony Thomas, 1997–2000

Rushing Yards: 4,645, Anthony Thomas, 1997–2000

Rushing Touchdowns: 55, Anthony Thomas, 1997–2000

Pass Attempts: 1,366, John Navarre, 2000–03

Pass Completions: 765, John Navarre, 2000–03

Passing Yards: 9,254, John Navarre, 2000–03

Passing Touchdowns: 72, John Navarre, 2000–03

Receptions: 252, Braylon Edwards, 2001–04

Receiving Yards: 3,541, Braylon Edwards, 2001–04

Touchdown Receptions: 39, Braylon Edwards, 2001–04

Punt Return Average (Min. 25): 17.1 yards, George Hoey, 1967–68

Kickoff Return Average (Min. 12): 26.9 yards, Desmond Howard, 1989–91

Total Tackles: 429, Jarrett Irons, 1993–96

Sacks: 28, Mark Messner, 1985–88

Tackles for Loss: 61, Mark Messner, 1985–88

Interceptions: 22, Tom Curtis, 1967–69

GAN STADIUM
D BLUE 13